ALL THE WAY DOWN
OCEAN

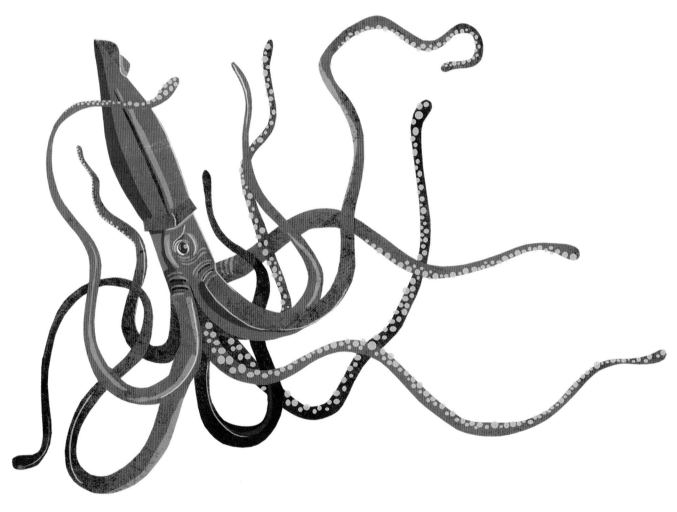

BOOK HOUSE
a SALARIYA *imprint*

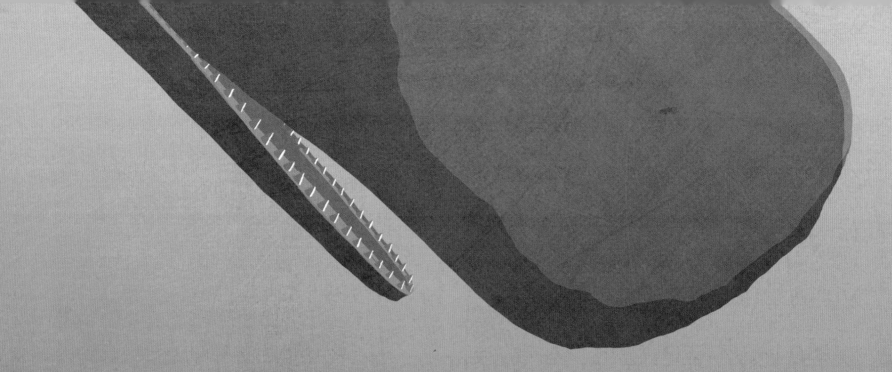

Author: Alex Woolf has written more than 150 books, both fiction and non-fiction, mostly for children. He has written on a huge range of subjects including Romans, chocolate, asteroids, sharks, Tudors, flying reptiles, soap, bees and acne. Many of these have sold around the world and his words have been translated into over a dozen different languages.

Illustrator: Isobel Lundie is an illustrator and designer who works in Brighton. Since graduating from Kingston University with a First-Class Honours in illustration and animation, she has specialised in children's publishing. Isobel has been lucky enough to make books for Salariya, Usborne, Random House, DK and the Good Book Company. She uses a wide variety of materials such as collage papers, pencil, ink and digital media. She likes creating detailed work with wacky characters that makes children laugh.

Consultant: Helen Lambert (née Proctor) BSc Hons, MSc, PhD (candidate) is an animal welfare scientist who is recognised around the world for her expertise and research into animal emotions. Helen has spent years working and researching for the charity sector, and she now runs her own consultancy business: Animal Welfare Consultancy.

Editor: Nick Pierce

This edition published in Great Britain in MMXXI
by Book House, an imprint of
The Salariya Book Company Ltd
25 Marlborough Place,
Brighton BN1 1UB
www.salariya.com

Text © Alex Woolf MMXXI
Illustrations © Isobel Lundie MMXXI
English language © The Salariya Book Company Ltd MMXXI
First published in MMXXI

Visit
www.salariya.com
for our online catalogue and
free fun stuff.

HB ISBN-13: 978-1-913337-83-4

1 3 5 7 9 8 6 4 2

A CIP catalogue record for this book is available from the British Library.

Printed and bound in China.

Printed on paper from sustainable sources.

ALL THE WAY DOWN
OCEAN

Written by Alex Woolf

Illustrated by Isobel Lundie

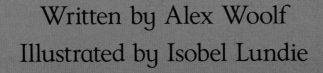

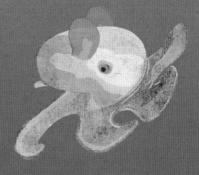

BOOK HOUSE
a SALARIYA *imprint*

CONTENTS

WHY ARE OUR OCEANS SO IMPORTANT?

1 THE OCEANS PRODUCE OVER HALF OF ALL THE OXYGEN WE BREATHE! MOST OF THIS IS CREATED BY PHYTOPLANKTON, A TINY MARINE ORGANISM THAT LIVES NEAR THE OCEAN SURFACE.

2 THEY ABSORB AROUND A QUARTER OF THE CARBON DIOXIDE WE EMIT WHEN WE BURN FOSSIL FUELS. SO IF IT WASN'T FOR THE OCEANS, GLOBAL WARMING WOULD BE MUCH WORSE.

3 THEY TRANSPORT HEAT FROM THE EQUATOR TO THE POLES, REGULATING OUR GLOBAL CLIMATE, TEMPERATURES AND WEATHER PATTERNS.

4 FINALLY, THE OCEANS ARE A DIVERSE ECOSYSTEM, HOME TO SOME 230,000 KNOWN SPECIES. WITH SO MUCH OF THE OCEAN STILL NOT FULLY EXPLORED, WHO KNOWS HOW MANY SPECIES WE HAVE YET TO DISCOVER!

SUNLIGHT ZONE
0–200 M (0–656 FEET)
90% of all ocean life lives here.

INTRODUCTION

There are five oceans on Earth – the Pacific, Atlantic, Indian, Southern and Arctic. Between them, they cover 71% of our planet's surface – that's around 362 million square kilometres (140 million square miles). As for the bottom of these oceans, we know very little about them. In fact, we have more detailed maps of the surface of Mars than we do of the ocean floor.

ZONES OF THE OCEAN

Scientists divide the ocean depths into five zones. Nearest the surface is the sunlight zone. Beneath that is the twilight zone, then the midnight zone, then the abyss, and finally, at the very bottom, the trenches. Each zone has different characteristics, including the light available, temperature, pressure and food sources. These characteristics influence the kinds of creatures that live there.

HOW TO USE THIS BOOK

In this book, you can journey all the way down to the bottom of the ocean, exploring each of these zones in turn. Discover the weird and wonderful animals that inhabit them and learn how they have adapted to their particular environment.

Have a good trip!

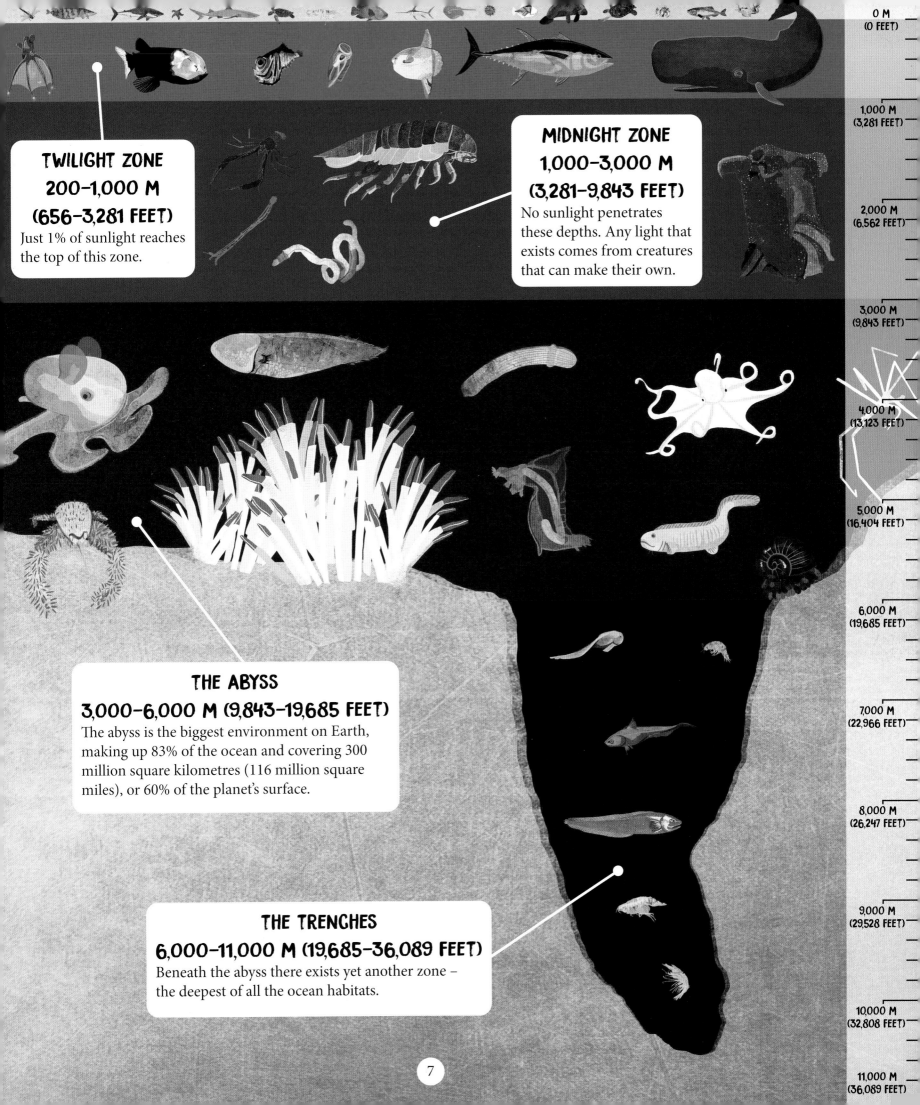

TWILIGHT ZONE
200–1,000 M
(656–3,281 FEET)

Just 1% of sunlight reaches the top of this zone.

MIDNIGHT ZONE
1,000–3,000 M
(3,281–9,843 FEET)

No sunlight penetrates these depths. Any light that exists comes from creatures that can make their own.

THE ABYSS
3,000–6,000 M (9,843–19,685 FEET)

The abyss is the biggest environment on Earth, making up 83% of the ocean and covering 300 million square kilometres (116 million square miles), or 60% of the planet's surface.

THE TRENCHES
6,000–11,000 M (19,685–36,089 FEET)

Beneath the abyss there exists yet another zone – the deepest of all the ocean habitats.

0 M (0 FEET)
1,000 M (3,281 FEET)
2,000 M (6,562 FEET)
3,000 M (9,843 FEET)
4,000 M (13,123 FEET)
5,000 M (16,404 FEET)
6,000 M (19,685 FEET)
7,000 M (22,966 FEET)
8,000 M (26,247 FEET)
9,000 M (29,528 FEET)
10,000 M (32,808 FEET)
11,000 M (36,089 FEET)

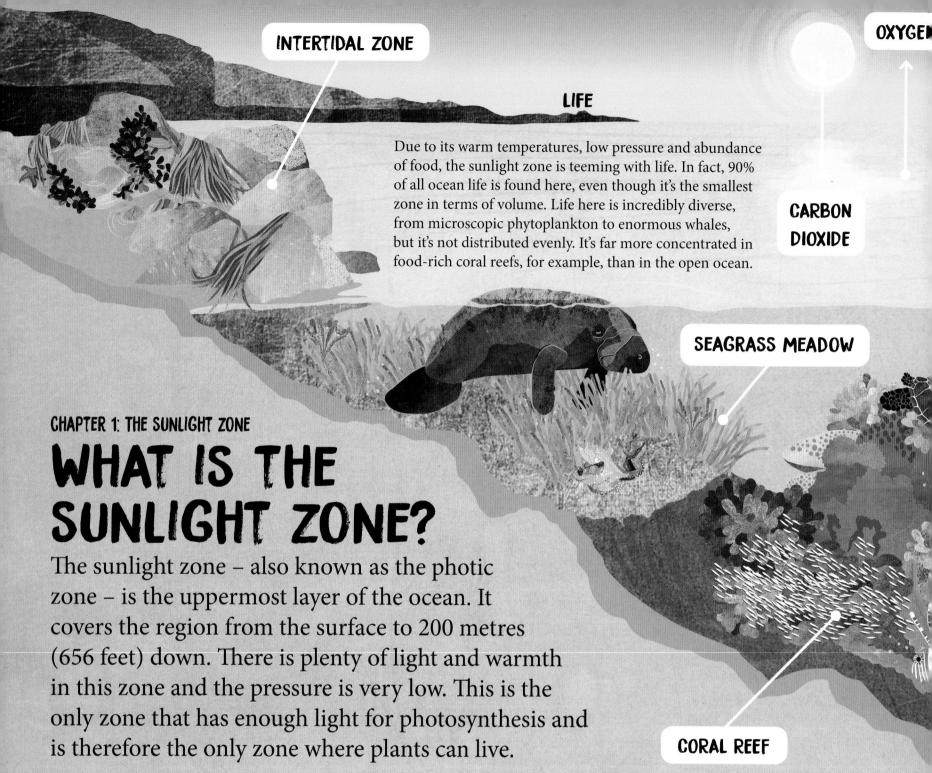

INTERTIDAL ZONE

LIFE

OXYGEN

Due to its warm temperatures, low pressure and abundance of food, the sunlight zone is teeming with life. In fact, 90% of all ocean life is found here, even though it's the smallest zone in terms of volume. Life here is incredibly diverse, from microscopic phytoplankton to enormous whales, but it's not distributed evenly. It's far more concentrated in food-rich coral reefs, for example, than in the open ocean.

CARBON DIOXIDE

SEAGRASS MEADOW

CHAPTER 1: THE SUNLIGHT ZONE

WHAT IS THE SUNLIGHT ZONE?

The sunlight zone – also known as the photic zone – is the uppermost layer of the ocean. It covers the region from the surface to 200 metres (656 feet) down. There is plenty of light and warmth in this zone and the pressure is very low. This is the only zone that has enough light for photosynthesis and is therefore the only zone where plants can live.

CORAL REEF

HABITATS

There are many different habitats within the sunlight zone, each varying in terms of temperature, depth and closeness to land. The habitat affects the kinds of creatures that live there. In this section, we'll be looking at the intertidal zone, estuaries, kelp forests, seagrass meadows, coral reefs and the open ocean.

THE INTERTIDAL ZONE

ESTUARIES

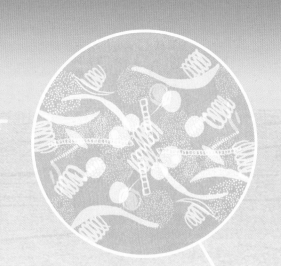

OPEN OCEAN

WHAT IS PHOTOSYNTHESIS AND WHY IS IT IMPORTANT IN OUR OCEANS?

Photosynthesis is a chemical process that takes place inside a plant. The plant takes light from the Sun and carbon dioxide from the atmosphere and converts them into food (to grow and reproduce), and oxygen. For photosynthesis to take place, plants need carbon dioxide, water and light – all of which are available in the sunlight zone.

PHYTOPLANKTON

At the base of the ocean's food chain are creatures too small for us to see: phytoplankton. Countless billions of these one-celled organisms live in the sunlight zone. They are eaten by animals that are, in turn, eaten by other animals. Phytoplankton thereby support all other marine life.

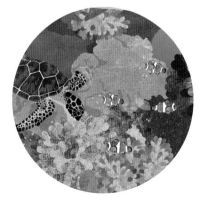

KELP FORESTS   SEAGRASS MEADOWS   CORAL REEFS   THE OPEN OCEAN

9

0 M
(0 FEET)

1,000 M
(3,281 FEET)

2,000 M
(6,562 FEET)

3,000 M
(9,843 FEET)

4,000 M
(13,123 FEET)

5,000 M
(16,404 FEET)

6,000 M
(19,685 FEET)

7,000 M
(22,966 FEET)

8,000 M
(26,247 FEET)

9,000 M
(29,528 FEET)

10,000 M
(32,808 FEET)

11,000 M
(36,089 FEET)

2. MUSSELS
Length: 5–10 cm (2–4 inches)
Depth range: 0–2,800 m (0–9,186 feet)

1. OCHRE STARFISH
Width: 15–35 cm (6–14 inches)
Depth range: 0–90 m (0–295 feet)

3. HERMIT CRAB
Length: averages 3.5 cm
(1.4 inches)
Depth range: 0–200 m
(0–656 feet)

4. BARNACLES
Width: 0.5–7 cm (0.2–3 inches)
Depth range: 0–600 m (0–1,968 feet)

5. PERIWINKLE SNAIL
Length: 1.5–3.8 cm (0.6–1.5 inches)
Depth range: 0–55 m (0–180 feet)

6. BLUESPOTTED RIBBONTAIL RAY
Length: up to 70 cm (2.3 feet)
Depth range: 0–30 m (0–98 feet)

THE INTERTIDAL ZONE

THE INTERTIDAL ZONE IS AN AREA OF THE COAST THAT IS UNDERWATER AT HIGH TIDE AND UNCOVERED DURING LOW TIDE. ANIMALS LIVING HERE MUST TOLERATE BEING COVERED BY SALTWATER AND ALSO BEING EXPOSED TO AIR AND SUNLIGHT, AS WELL AS ROUGH WAVES. INTERTIDAL SPECIES HAVE DEVELOPED DIFFERENT ADAPTATIONS TO COPE WITH THESE CHALLENGING CONDITIONS.

1 OCHRE STARFISH Ochre starfishes can tolerate up to eight hours exposed to air at low tide. They feed on mussels, snails and barnacles, and are known as a 'keystone species' because they help maintain a diverse intertidal community.

2 MUSSELS Mussels live in a narrow band of the intertidal zone. Too far from the sea, they cannot get enough food; too close and they fall prey to sea stars. They group together in clusters to reduce each one's exposure to sunlight, so that they don't dry up.

3 HERMIT CRAB The hermit crab lives in a shell scavenged from other creatures, such as sea snails. The shell stores water and shelters the crab from the Sun during low tide.

4 BARNACLES Barnacles survive the strong waves by anchoring themselves to rocks. During low tide they close their shells to stop their moist bodies from drying up. Their shells are made up of hard plates that protect them from predators.

5 PERIWINKLE SNAIL When the tide is low, periwinkles excrete a mucus that traps the water in their shell to prevent them from drying out. The mucus also glues them to the rock so they don't get pulled out to sea.

6 BLUESPOTTED RIBBONTAIL RAY At night, as the tide rises, bluespotted ribbontail rays gather in groups and swim onto the sandy flats of the intertidal zone to feed. They dig into the sandy bed in search of molluscs, worms, shrimps and crabs.

0 M (0 FEET)
1,000 M (3,281 FEET)
2,000 M (6,562 FEET)
3,000 M (9,843 FEET)
4,000 M (13,123 FEET)
5,000 M (16,404 FEET)
6,000 M (19,685 FEET)
7,000 M (22,966 FEET)
8,000 M (26,247 FEET)
9,000 M (29,528 FEET)
10,000 M (32,808 FEET)
11,000 M (36,089 FEET)

1. GREAT BLUE HERON
Length: about 97–140 cm (3–4.6 feet)
Depth range: 0–50 cm (0–1.5 feet)

2. COMMON SNAPPING TURTLE
Length: 25–46 cm shell (1–1.5 feet)
Depth range: 0–1 m (0–3 feet)

3. HARBOUR SEAL
Length: 1.85 m (6.1 feet)
Depth range: 0–500 m (0–1,640 feet)

4. SALMON
Length: 36–46 cm (1–1.5 feet)
Depth range: 0–118 m
(0–387 feet)

5. DRAGONFLY
Length: 2.5–13 cm
(1–5 inches)
Depth range: 0 m
(0 feet)

6. STARRY FLOUNDER
Length: up to 60 cm (2 feet)
Depth range: 0–375 m
(0–1,230 feet)

ESTUARIES

ESTUARIES ARE COASTAL AREAS WHERE RIVERS MEET THE SEA. THE WATER IS BRACKISH – PART FRESH, PART SALTY. ESTUARIES ARE WELL-PROTECTED, WITH FEW WAVES, MAKING THEM IDEAL FOR MARINE ANIMALS TO RAISE THEIR YOUNG. TIDAL MOVEMENTS AND THE ABUNDANCE OF PLANT LIFE CREATE A WEALTH OF FOOD FOR ANIMALS LIVING THERE. ESTUARY ANIMALS RANGE FROM TINY PLANKTON TO ENORMOUS WHALES.

1 GREAT BLUE HERON This large, long-legged bird lives around estuary marshes and mudflats, feeding on fish, shrimp, crabs, aquatic insects, small mammals and birds. It hunts by wading slowly through shallow water and spearing its prey with its long, sharp bill.

2 COMMON SNAPPING TURTLE This turtle lives in ponds, streams and estuaries. It often lies on the muddy bottom with only its head exposed. It eats plants and small fish, frogs, reptiles and birds.

3 HARBOUR SEAL Harbour seals frequently gather in groups around estuaries in search of prey fish such as salmon, sea bass, herring and cod. They spend about half their lives on land, resting on rocky areas and sandbanks close to their feeding sites.

4 SALMON Salmon are born in rivers, then make their way to the ocean. Estuaries play a vital role in this life cycle. Salmon spend a year or more in their brackish waters preparing themselves for the salty sea. At the end of their lives, salmon return to the estuary before heading upriver to spawn.

5 DRAGONFLY The dragonfly is a very common estuary insect. It starts life underwater as a dragonfly nymph, eating tadpoles and fish eggs. Adults consume other aquatic insects by capturing them while flying.

6 STARRY FLOUNDER Starry flounders lay their eggs in estuaries. They cannot tolerate very salty water, so spend their lives in brackish estuary waters, occasionally venturing upriver into fresh water. As a defence, they change colour to blend in with the sandy or muddy estuary bottom.

0 M (0 FEET)
1,000 M (3,281 FEET)
2,000 M (6,562 FEET)
3,000 M (9,843 FEET)
4,000 M (13,123 FEET)
5,000 M (16,404 FEET)
6,000 M (19,685 FEET)
7,000 M (22,966 FEET)
8,000 M (26,247 FEET)
9,000 M (29,528 FEET)
10,000 M (32,808 FEET)
11,000 M (36,089 FEET)

1. SEA OTTER
Length: 1.2–1.5 m (4–5 feet)
Depth range: 0–90 m (0–295 feet)

2. PURPLE SEA URCHIN
Width: up to 10 cm (4 inches)
Depth range: 0–160 m (0–525 feet)

3. GIANT KELPFISH
Length: up to 61 cm (2 feet)
Depth range: 0–40 m
(0–131 feet)

4. KELP
Height: up to 30–80 m (98–262 feet)
Depth range: 2–30 m (7–98 feet)

5. GREY WHALE
Length: up to 12 m (40 feet)
Depth range: 0–155 m (0–509 feet)

6. KELP ROCKFISH
Length: up to 43 cm (1.4 feet)
Depth range: 0–42 m (0–138 feet)

15

KELP FORESTS

KELP FORESTS GROW IN COLD, CLEAR, SHALLOW COASTAL WATERS. THEY ARE FOUND MAINLY ON ROCKY COASTLINES, SUCH AS IN NORWAY OR ON THE PACIFIC COAST OF NORTH AMERICA. DURING STORMS, MANY ANIMALS RETREAT TO KELP FORESTS FOR SHELTER. THE FORESTS ALSO ACT AS A SAFE SPACE FOR ANIMALS TO RAISE THEIR YOUNG AND SEEK REFUGE FROM LARGER PREDATORS.

1 SEA OTTER Sea otters eat purple sea urchins, a major threat to kelp forests, helping to conserve the habitat. Sea otters wrap themselves in ribbons of kelp to anchor themselves so they don't drift into deeper water while sleeping.

2 PURPLE SEA URCHIN Purple sea urchins live in the kelp forests along the eastern edge of the Pacific, and their main diet is kelp. Since 2014, their population has exploded, partly because of the effects of climate change. This has caused the disappearance of large areas of kelp forest off the western coast of North America.

3 GIANT KELPFISH The giant kelpfish lives in rocky areas where kelp grows, off the western coast of North America. It eats the small fishes, crustaceans and molluscs living there. Its elongated body is shaped like a kelp blade for camouflage. Its eggs are sticky so they attach to the kelp.

4 KELP Kelp is a large, brown algae – a type of seaweed. It has a long, tough stalk with broad, leaflike structures called blades, and is anchored to the seabed by a clawlike growth called a holdfast. It can grow very fast – up to half a metre a day!

5 GREY WHALE Grey whales, migrating from Baja California to their feeding grounds in Alaska, use kelp forests as a refuge to keep their calves safe from their major predator, the killer whale. They feed on the many small animals that live there.

6 KELP ROCKFISH The kelp rockfish eats the small fishes, shrimps and other crustaceans that inhabit the kelp forest. It does most of its hunting at night. During the day it commonly rests on a kelp blade, sometimes upside down.

0 M
(0 FEET)

1,000 M
(3,281 FEET)

2,000 M
(6,562 FEET)

3,000 M
(9,843 FEET)

4,000 M
(13,123 FEET)

5,000 M
(16,404 FEET)

6,000 M
(19,685 FEET)

7,000 M
(22,966 FEET)

8,000 M
(26,247 FEET)

9,000 M
(29,528 FEET)

10,000 M
(32,808 FEET)

11,000 M
(36,089 FEET)

1. MANATEE
Length: 2.8–3 m (9–10 feet)
Depth range: 0–10 m (0–33 feet)

2. STALKED JELLYFISH
Length: 2 cm (1 inch)
Depth range: 0–21 m (0–69 feet)

3. ALGAE OCTOPUS
Length: 25 cm (10 inch) legs
Depth range: 0–1 m (0–3 feet)

4. SPONGE
Length: up to 2 m (6.5 feet)
Depth range: 0–8,500 m (0–27,887 feet)

5. GREEN SEA TURTLE
Length: 1–1.2 m (3–4 feet)
Depth range: 0–21 m (0–69 feet)

6. SHRIMP
Length: 4–8 cm (2–3 inches)
Depth range: 0–1.5 m (0–5 feet)

SEAGRASS MEADOWS

IN SHALLOW COASTAL SEAS THROUGHOUT THE WORLD, SEAGRASSES CAN BE FOUND. SEAGRASSES HAVE ROOTS, STEMS AND LEAVES JUST LIKE PLANTS ON LAND. THERE ARE AROUND 72 SEAGRASS SPECIES AND THEY GROW IN DENSE UNDERWATER MEADOWS, SOME BIG ENOUGH TO BE SEEN FROM SPACE. THEY PROVIDE SHELTER AND FOOD FOR A DIVERSE RANGE OF ANIMALS.

1 MANATEE Manatees, also known as sea cows, are perfectly adapted to their seagrass-meadow habitat. They graze in the shallow waters, using their flippers to move along or to dig up the grass and move it to their lips. The lips have special muscles to manipulate and tear up the grass.

2 STALKED JELLYFISH This unusual jellyfish spends its life attached to rocks or seagrass. Its umbrella-shaped body has eight stinging tentacles pointing upwards, which it uses to catch passing prey.

3 ALGAE OCTOPUS The algae octopus lives in dens in the sandy seafloor near seagrass meadows, where it feeds on small crabs. As part of its defence against predators, the octopus will camouflage itself to look like a shell covered in algae.

4 SPONGE Sponges, which nestle between blades of seagrass, release nitrogen, a nutrient that seagrasses need to grow. Sponges are also an important prey for fish, sharks and turtles hunting in the meadows.

5 GREEN SEA TURTLE Adult green sea turtles spend much of their lives grazing in seagrass meadows, and they play an important role in keeping the meadows healthy. By trimming off the tips of the blades with their serrated beaks, they improve the growth of the seagrass, while leaving the roots completely undisturbed.

6 SHRIMP Some species of shrimp not only eat seagrass, but also use it as a building material. The thalassinid shrimps of Indonesia tear seagrass leaves off their stems, cut them into pieces and use them to line their underground burrows.

0 M (0 FEET)
1,000 M (3,281 FEET)
2,000 M (6,562 FEET)
3,000 M (9,843 FEET)
4,000 M (13,123 FEET)
5,000 M (16,404 FEET)
6,000 M (19,685 FEET)
7,000 M (22,966 FEET)
8,000 M (26,247 FEET)
9,000 M (29,528 FEET)
10,000 M (32,808 FEET)
11,000 M (36,089 FEET)

1. PICASSO TRIGGER FISH
Length: 25–30 cm (10–12 inches)
Depth range: 0–50 m (0–164 feet)

3. NAPOLEON WRASSE
Length: up to 2 m (6.5 feet)
Depth range: 0–61 m (0–200 feet)

2. WHITETIP REEF SHARK
Length: up to 1.5 m (5 feet)
Depth range: 0–330 m (0–1,082 feet)

4. HAWKSBILL SEA TURTLE
Length: 71–89 cm (2.5–3 feet)
Depth range: 0–175 m (0–574 feet)

5. CLOWNFISH
Length: 11 cm (4 inches)
Depth range: 0–12 m
(0–40 feet)

18

6. LIONFISH
Length: up to 33 cm (1 foot)
Depth range: 0–300 m (0–984 feet)

CORAL REEFS

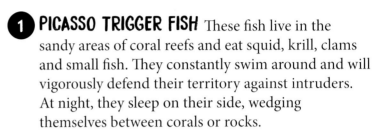

CORAL REEFS COVER LESS THAN 1% OF THE OCEAN BUT ARE HOME TO AROUND A QUARTER OF ALL MARINE SPECIES! THEY ARE MADE OF LAYERS OF A HARD MATERIAL, CALCIUM CARBONATE, SECRETED BY TINY ANIMALS CALLED CORAL POLYPS. CORAL REEFS HOST AN INCREDIBLY DIVERSE RANGE OF ANIMALS, INCLUDING SPONGES, CRUSTACEANS, MOLLUSCS, FISH, TURTLES, SHARKS, DOLPHINS AND MANY MORE.

1 PICASSO TRIGGER FISH These fish live in the sandy areas of coral reefs and eat squid, krill, clams and small fish. They constantly swim around and will vigorously defend their territory against intruders. At night, they sleep on their side, wedging themselves between corals or rocks.

2 WHITETIP REEF SHARK Whitetip reef sharks lurk hungrily around coral reefs, hunting eels, fish, octopuses and crabs. Their slim, agile bodies can wriggle into narrow crevices in the reef to extract prey. They feed mainly at night, sometimes teaming up to block a prey's exit route from the reef.

3 NAPOLEON WRASSE The Napoleon wrasse is one of the largest fish in the coral reef. It swims in the outer reef during the day, feeding on molluscs, reef fish, sea urchins and crustaceans. At night it sleeps in reef caves or below coral ledges.

4 HAWKSBILL SEA TURTLE Adult hawksbills are found mainly in tropical coral reefs. They feed on sponges, using their narrow, pointed beaks to extract them from crevices. By removing sponges from the coral, they give better access to reef fish to feed.

5 CLOWNFISH Clownfish make their home amid the stinging tentacles of the sea anemone. The clownfish is immune to the stingers, and the anemone offers protection against predators. In return, the clownfish keeps the anemone healthy and clean.

6 LIONFISH Lionfish are aggressive predators of smaller fish, and can harm coral reefs if their numbers get too large. Their prey eat algae from the coral, and if the lionfish eat too many of them, the algae grows unchecked, which can damage the health of the reef.

0 M (0 FEET)

1,000 M (3,281 FEET)

2,000 M (6,562 FEET)

3,000 M (9,843 FEET)

4,000 M (13,123 FEET)

5,000 M (16,404 FEET)

6,000 M (19,685 FEET)

7,000 M (22,966 FEET)

8,000 M (26,247 FEET)

9,000 M (29,528 FEET)

10,000 M (32,808 FEET)

11,000 M (36,089 FEET)

1. FLYING FISH
Length: up to 46 cm (1.5 feet)
Depth range: 0–200 m (0–656 feet)

3. WHALE SHARK
Length: 5.5–10 m (18–33 feet)
Depth range: 0–1,800 m
(0–5,906 feet)

2. SWORDFISH
Length: up to 3 m (10 feet)
Depth range: 0–550 m
(0–1,804 feet)

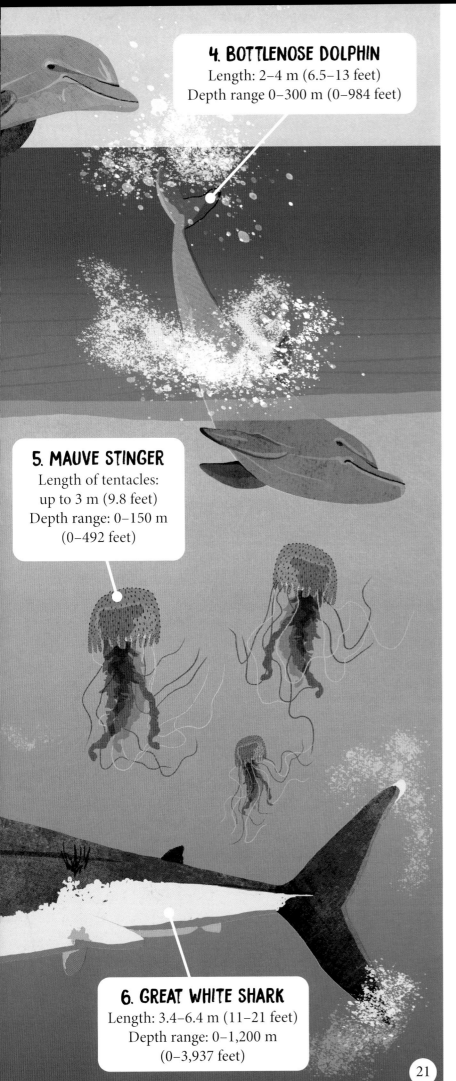

4. BOTTLENOSE DOLPHIN
Length: 2–4 m (6.5–13 feet)
Depth range 0–300 m (0–984 feet)

5. MAUVE STINGER
Length of tentacles:
up to 3 m (9.8 feet)
Depth range: 0–150 m
(0–492 feet)

6. GREAT WHITE SHARK
Length: 3.4–6.4 m (11–21 feet)
Depth range: 0–1,200 m
(0–3,937 feet)

THE OPEN OCEAN

THE OPEN OCEAN IS BY FAR THE LARGEST HABITAT IN THE SUNLIGHT ZONE. IT LIES BEYOND THE COASTAL AREAS AND EXTENDS FROM THE POLAR REGIONS TO THE TROPICS. CREATURES LIVING HERE SPEND THEIR ENTIRE LIVES SURROUNDED BY WATER ON ALL SIDES. SOME ANIMALS, LIKE PLANKTON, DRIFT ON THE CURRENTS. OTHERS, LIKE WHALES, DOLPHINS AND SHARKS, SWIM LONG DISTANCES.

1 FLYING FISH Flying fish have evolved their own unique way of escaping predators in the open ocean – by opening their long, wing-shaped fins and gliding above the waves. Most flights are around 50 metres (164 feet), but by catching updrafts of wind they can achieve distances of up to 400 metres (1,312 feet).

2 SWORDFISH Like all open ocean dwellers, swordfish are agile swimmers with streamlined bodies and are capable of long-distance journeys. Swordfish migrate to colder regions to feed in summer. They are very fast when hunting, using their 'sword' to slash at prey.

3 WHALE SHARK The whale shark is the largest fish in the world. Yet it is a peaceful animal, feeding on plankton and small fish. It filters them from the water, which it sucks into its enormous mouth. The shark lives in warm parts of the open ocean.

4 BOTTLENOSE DOLPHIN These dolphins live in groups for hunting and self-defence in the vast ocean. They find their prey by means of echolocation, and make high-pitched whistles and squeaks to alert the group to nearby food or approaching danger.

5 MAUVE STINGER Unlike most jellyfish, the mauve stinger spends its entire life in the deep ocean, so it doesn't have a bottom-dwelling polyp stage in its life cycle. Spending its life in this vast, nutrient-poor habitat, it feeds on any small organism it comes across.

6 GREAT WHITE SHARK Each year, great white sharks migrate up to 4,000 kilometres (2,485 miles) across the Pacific to reach their feeding grounds. They use oil stored in their livers as a source of energy on these epic journeys. The oil keeps them buoyant, so by the end of the journey they are heavier in the water.

0 M
(0 FEET)

1,000 M
(3,281 FEET)

2,000 M
(6,562 FEET)

3,000 M
(9,843 FEET)

4,000 M
(13,123 FEET)

5,000 M
(16,404 FEET)

6,000 M
(19,685 FEET)

7,000 M
(22,966 FEET)

8,000 M
(26,247 FEET)

9,000 M
(29,528 FEET)

10,000 M
(32,808 FEET)

11,000 M
(36,089 FEET)

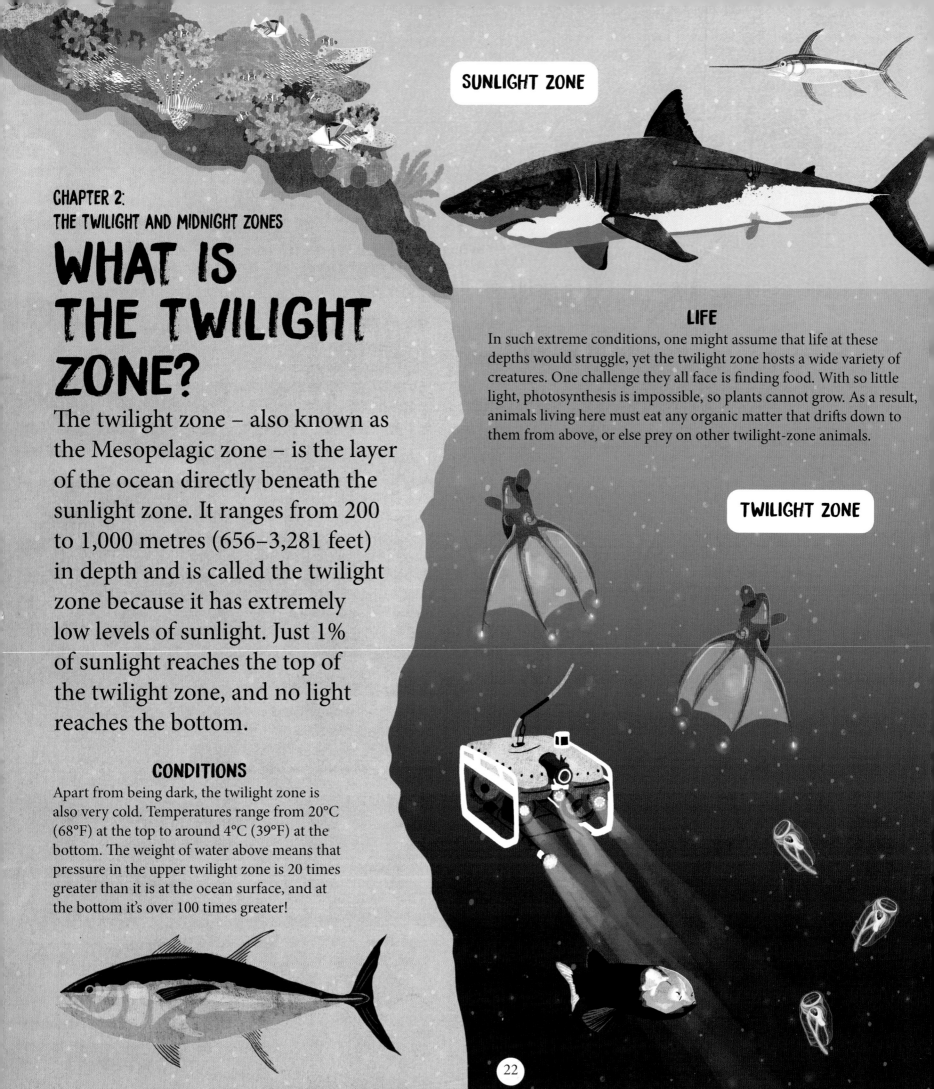

SUNLIGHT ZONE

CHAPTER 2:
THE TWILIGHT AND MIDNIGHT ZONES
WHAT IS THE TWILIGHT ZONE?

The twilight zone – also known as the Mesopelagic zone – is the layer of the ocean directly beneath the sunlight zone. It ranges from 200 to 1,000 metres (656–3,281 feet) in depth and is called the twilight zone because it has extremely low levels of sunlight. Just 1% of sunlight reaches the top of the twilight zone, and no light reaches the bottom.

CONDITIONS

Apart from being dark, the twilight zone is also very cold. Temperatures range from 20°C (68°F) at the top to around 4°C (39°F) at the bottom. The weight of water above means that pressure in the upper twilight zone is 20 times greater than it is at the ocean surface, and at the bottom it's over 100 times greater!

LIFE

In such extreme conditions, one might assume that life at these depths would struggle, yet the twilight zone hosts a wide variety of creatures. One challenge they all face is finding food. With so little light, photosynthesis is impossible, so plants cannot grow. As a result, animals living here must eat any organic matter that drifts down to them from above, or else prey on other twilight-zone animals.

TWILIGHT ZONE

UNDER PRESSURE

To cope with the high pressure, creatures living in the twilight zone can have no gas-filled spaces in their body such as lungs or swim bladders. They tend to have jelly-like flesh with few bones. Animals found at these depths include jellyfish, sea cucumbers, shrimps, squid, sponges and some strange-looking fish. We'll meet a few of them on the following pages.

MIGRATION

Another option for twilight-zone animals is to travel into the sunlight zone to feed, and that is what many of them do. Each night, billions of twilight-zone dwellers swim up to surface waters to feed under cover of darkness. They return to the relative safety of deeper waters at daybreak to avoid becoming food themselves. This is the largest animal migration on the planet.

0 M
(0 FEET)

1,000 M
(3,281 FEET)

2,000 M
(6,562 FEET)

3,000 M
(9,843 FEET)

4,000 M
(13,123 FEET)

5,000 M
(16,404 FEET)

6,000 M
(19,685 FEET)

7,000 M
(22,966 FEET)

8,000 M
(26,247 FEET)

9,000 M
(29,528 FEET)

10,000 M
(32,808 FEET)

11,000 M
(36,089 FEET)

1. BIGEYE TUNA
Length: up to 2.5 m (8 feet)
Depth range: 0–500 m (0–1,640 feet)

2. SABRETOOTH FISH
Length: up to 18.5 cm (7 inches)
Depth range: 200–1,000 m
(656–3,281 feet)

3. SPERM WHALE
Length: up to 12 m (39 feet)
Depth range: 0–1,000 m
(0–3,281 feet)

4. BARRELEYE
Length: under 10 cm (3.9 inches)
Depth range: 400–2,500 m (1,312–8,202 feet)

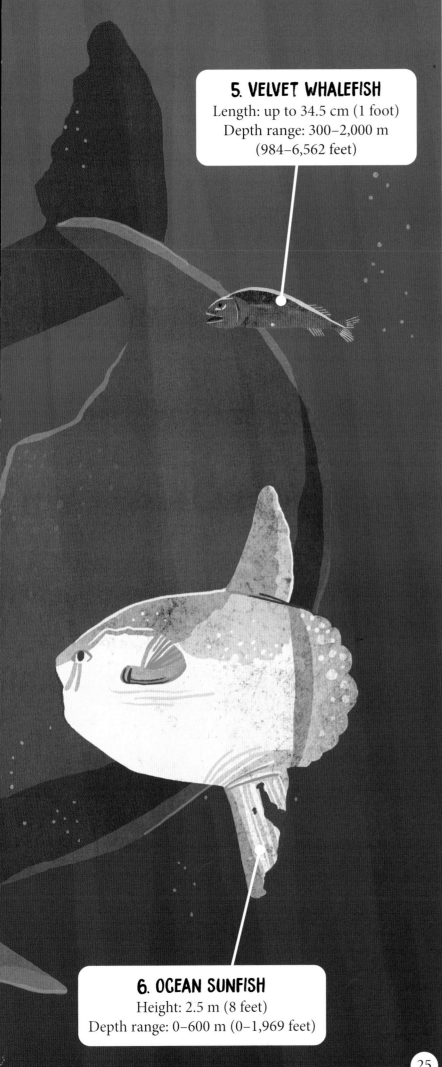

5. VELVET WHALEFISH
Length: up to 34.5 cm (1 foot)
Depth range: 300–2,000 m
(984–6,562 feet)

6. OCEAN SUNFISH
Height: 2.5 m (8 feet)
Depth range: 0–600 m (0–1,969 feet)

TWILIGHT-ZONE PREDATORS

VISITORS FROM THE SUNLIGHT ZONE DIVE DEEP TO HUNT HERE. THEIR BODIES ARE SPECIALLY ADAPTED TO WITHSTAND THE HUGE PRESSURES. THERE ARE ALSO PREDATORS THAT PERMANENTLY INHABIT THE DARK DEPTHS. THEIR EYES ARE ALWAYS LOOKING UP, TRYING TO GLIMPSE PREY SILHOUETTED AGAINST THE DIM LIGHT FROM THE SURFACE.

1 BIGEYE TUNA Bigeye tuna are uniquely adapted to hunt in the upper twilight zone. Their bodies can cope with the lower oxygen levels and stay warm despite the cold temperatures. Their large eyes give them good vision in the low-light conditions.

2 SABRETOOTH FISH These fish have upward-pointed eyes, adapted for picking out prey silhouetted against the dim waters above. With their big jaws and expandable stomachs, they can catch and eat prey bigger than themselves – useful, as meals can be rare.

3 SPERM WHALE Sperm whales can dive to great depths in search of prey such as giant squid. They can withstand the pressures by collapsing their lungs (thanks to a flexible ribcage) and decreasing their heart rate to preserve oxygen supplies.

4 BARRELEYE These fish have barrel-shaped eyes inside their transparent heads. The eyes mostly point upwards to catch silhouettes of prey, but can also rotate forwards. They eat zooplankton and small species of crustaceans.

5 VELVET WHALEFISH This deep-sea hunter makes nightly vertical migrations to the twilight zone to prey on small crustaceans. Whalefish have big eyes to see better in the dark waters. Their bright red colour makes them invisible to most other twilight-zone dwellers.

6 OCEAN SUNFISH The largest bony fish in the world, it has a strange, almost circular shape because the tail fin never grows. It hunts jellyfish, small fish and crustaceans in the chilly twilight zone, then returns to the surface to bask in the sun and get warm again.

0 M
(0 FEET)

1,000 M
(3,281 FEET)

2,000 M
(6,562 FEET)

3,000 M
(9,843 FEET)

4,000 M
(13,123 FEET)

5,000 M
(16,404 FEET)

6,000 M
(19,685 FEET)

7,000 M
(22,966 FEET)

8,000 M
(26,247 FEET)

9,000 M
(29,528 FEET)

10,000 M
(32,808 FEET)

11,000 M
(36,089 FEET)

1. HUMPBACK ANGLERFISH
Length: up to 18 cm (7 inches) (female)
Depth range: 100–1,500 m (328–4,921 feet)

2. DEEP-SEA HATCHETFISH
Length: up to 12 cm (5 inches)
Depth range: 50–1,500 m
(164–4,921 feet)

3. SALP
Length: 1–10 cm
(0.5–4 inches)
Depth range: 0–800 m
(0–2,625 feet)

4. VAMPIRE SQUID
Length: 28 cm (11 inches)
Depth range: 90–900 m
(295–2,953 feet)

5. STOPLIGHT LOOSEJAW
Length: up to 30 cm (1 foot)
Depth range: below 500 m (1,640 feet)

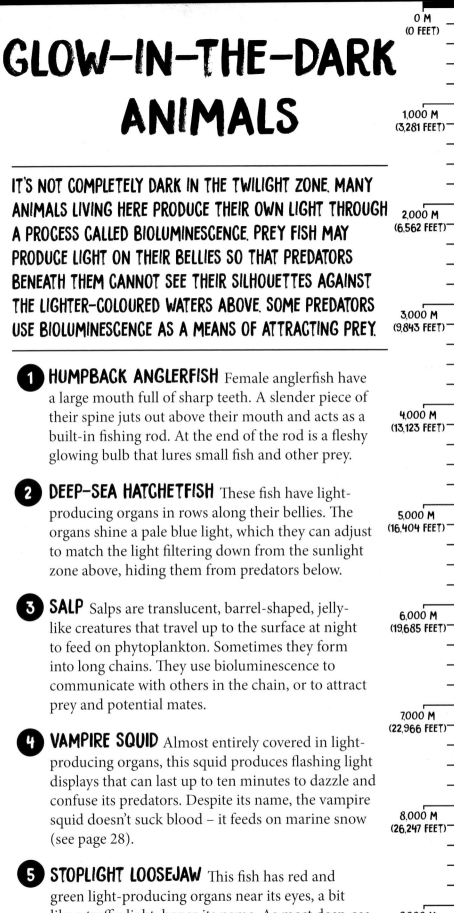

GLOW-IN-THE-DARK ANIMALS

It's not completely dark in the twilight zone. Many animals living here produce their own light through a process called bioluminescence. Prey fish may produce light on their bellies so that predators beneath them cannot see their silhouettes against the lighter-coloured waters above. Some predators use bioluminescence as a means of attracting prey.

1 HUMPBACK ANGLERFISH Female anglerfish have a large mouth full of sharp teeth. A slender piece of their spine juts out above their mouth and acts as a built-in fishing rod. At the end of the rod is a fleshy glowing bulb that lures small fish and other prey.

2 DEEP-SEA HATCHETFISH These fish have light-producing organs in rows along their bellies. The organs shine a pale blue light, which they can adjust to match the light filtering down from the sunlight zone above, hiding them from predators below.

3 SALP Salps are translucent, barrel-shaped, jelly-like creatures that travel up to the surface at night to feed on phytoplankton. Sometimes they form into long chains. They use bioluminescence to communicate with others in the chain, or to attract prey and potential mates.

4 VAMPIRE SQUID Almost entirely covered in light-producing organs, this squid produces flashing light displays that can last up to ten minutes to dazzle and confuse its predators. Despite its name, the vampire squid doesn't suck blood – it feeds on marine snow (see page 28).

5 STOPLIGHT LOOSEJAW This fish has red and green light-producing organs near its eyes, a bit like a traffic light, hence its name. As most deep-sea creatures cannot perceive the colour red, it is able to hunt quite stealthily.

6 ATOLLA JELLYFISH The deep red light of this jellyfish makes it invisible to its predators. When touched, the atolla flashes bright blue circles of light. These attract larger species of predators, scaring away its attacker.

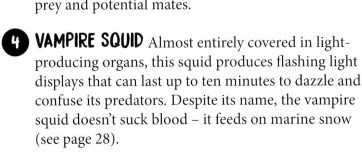

6. ATOLLA JELLYFISH
Width: 25 cm (10 inches) in diameter
Depth range: 500–1,000 m (1,640–3,281 feet)

0 M (0 FEET)
1,000 M (3,281 FEET)
2,000 M (6,562 FEET)
3,000 M (9,843 FEET)
4,000 M (13,123 FEET)
5,000 M (16,404 FEET)
6,000 M (19,685 FEET)
7,000 M (22,966 FEET)
8,000 M (26,247 FEET)
9,000 M (29,528 FEET)
10,000 M (32,808 FEET)
11,000 M (36,089 FEET)

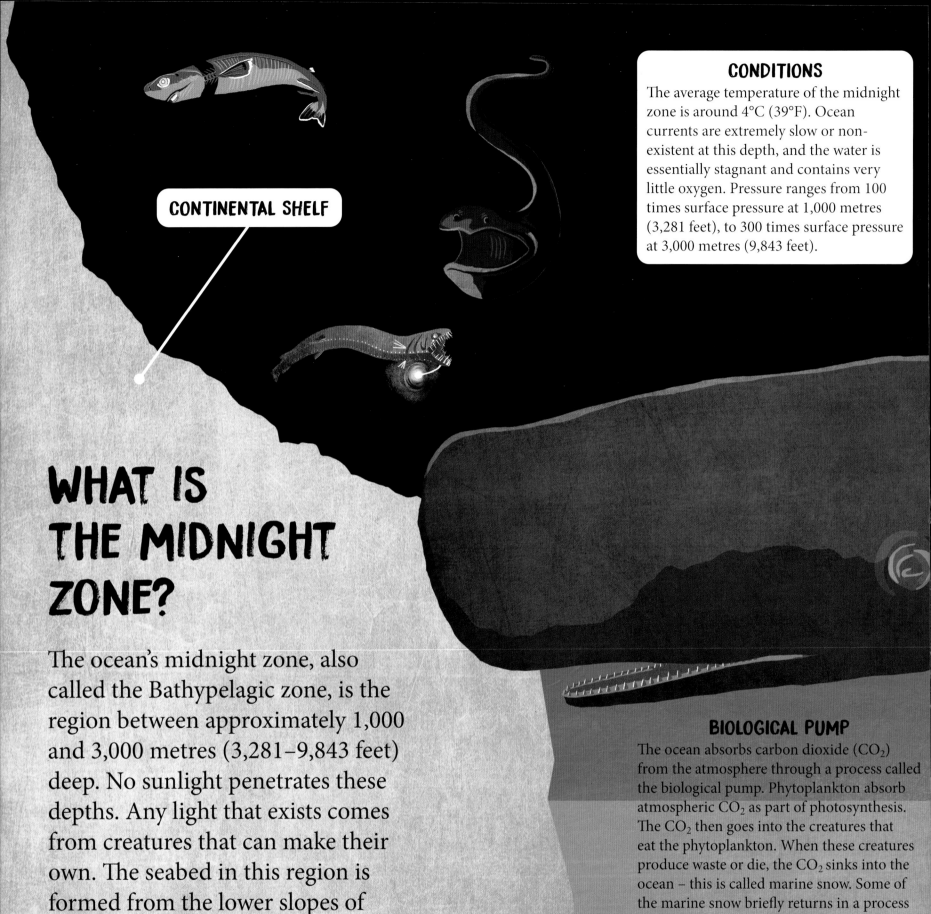

CONTINENTAL SHELF

CONDITIONS

The average temperature of the midnight zone is around 4°C (39°F). Ocean currents are extremely slow or non-existent at this depth, and the water is essentially stagnant and contains very little oxygen. Pressure ranges from 100 times surface pressure at 1,000 metres (3,281 feet), to 300 times surface pressure at 3,000 metres (9,843 feet).

WHAT IS THE MIDNIGHT ZONE?

The ocean's midnight zone, also called the Bathypelagic zone, is the region between approximately 1,000 and 3,000 metres (3,281–9,843 feet) deep. No sunlight penetrates these depths. Any light that exists comes from creatures that can make their own. The seabed in this region is formed from the lower slopes of continental shelves and seamounts rising up from the abyss.

BIOLOGICAL PUMP

The ocean absorbs carbon dioxide (CO_2) from the atmosphere through a process called the biological pump. Phytoplankton absorb atmospheric CO_2 as part of photosynthesis. The CO_2 then goes into the creatures that eat the phytoplankton. When these creatures produce waste or die, the CO_2 sinks into the ocean – this is called marine snow. Some of the marine snow briefly returns in a process called upwelling, as currents bring deeper, cooler waters to the surface. However, all marine snow eventually ends up on the seafloor, and this is how the ocean lowers the amount of CO_2 in the atmosphere.

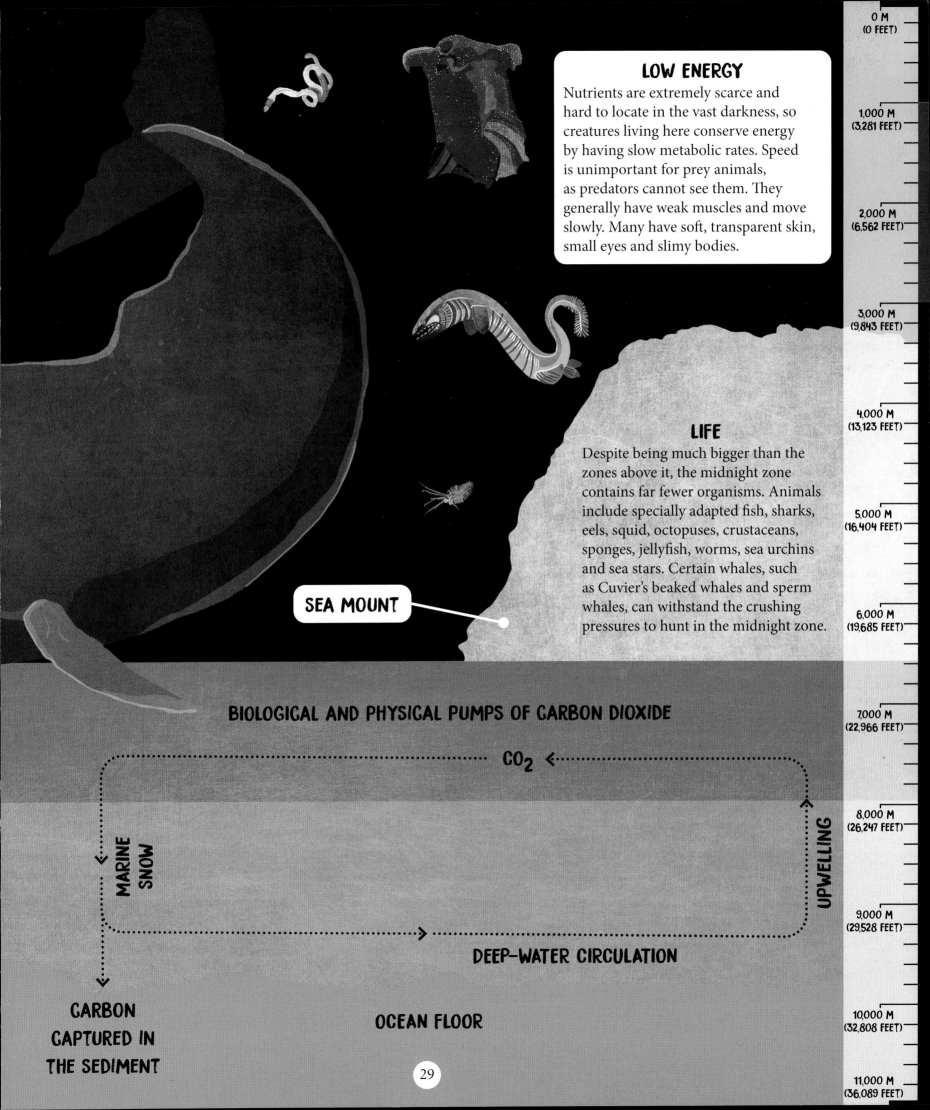

LOW ENERGY

Nutrients are extremely scarce and hard to locate in the vast darkness, so creatures living here conserve energy by having slow metabolic rates. Speed is unimportant for prey animals, as predators cannot see them. They generally have weak muscles and move slowly. Many have soft, transparent skin, small eyes and slimy bodies.

LIFE

Despite being much bigger than the zones above it, the midnight zone contains far fewer organisms. Animals include specially adapted fish, sharks, eels, squid, octopuses, crustaceans, sponges, jellyfish, worms, sea urchins and sea stars. Certain whales, such as Cuvier's beaked whales and sperm whales, can withstand the crushing pressures to hunt in the midnight zone.

SEA MOUNT

BIOLOGICAL AND PHYSICAL PUMPS OF CARBON DIOXIDE

CO_2

MARINE SNOW

UPWELLING

DEEP-WATER CIRCULATION

CARBON CAPTURED IN THE SEDIMENT

OCEAN FLOOR

0 M	(0 FEET)
1,000 M	(3,281 FEET)
2,000 M	(6,562 FEET)
3,000 M	(9,843 FEET)
4,000 M	(13,123 FEET)
5,000 M	(16,404 FEET)
6,000 M	(19,685 FEET)
7,000 M	(22,966 FEET)
8,000 M	(26,247 FEET)
9,000 M	(29,528 FEET)
10,000 M	(32,808 FEET)
11,000 M	(36,089 FEET)

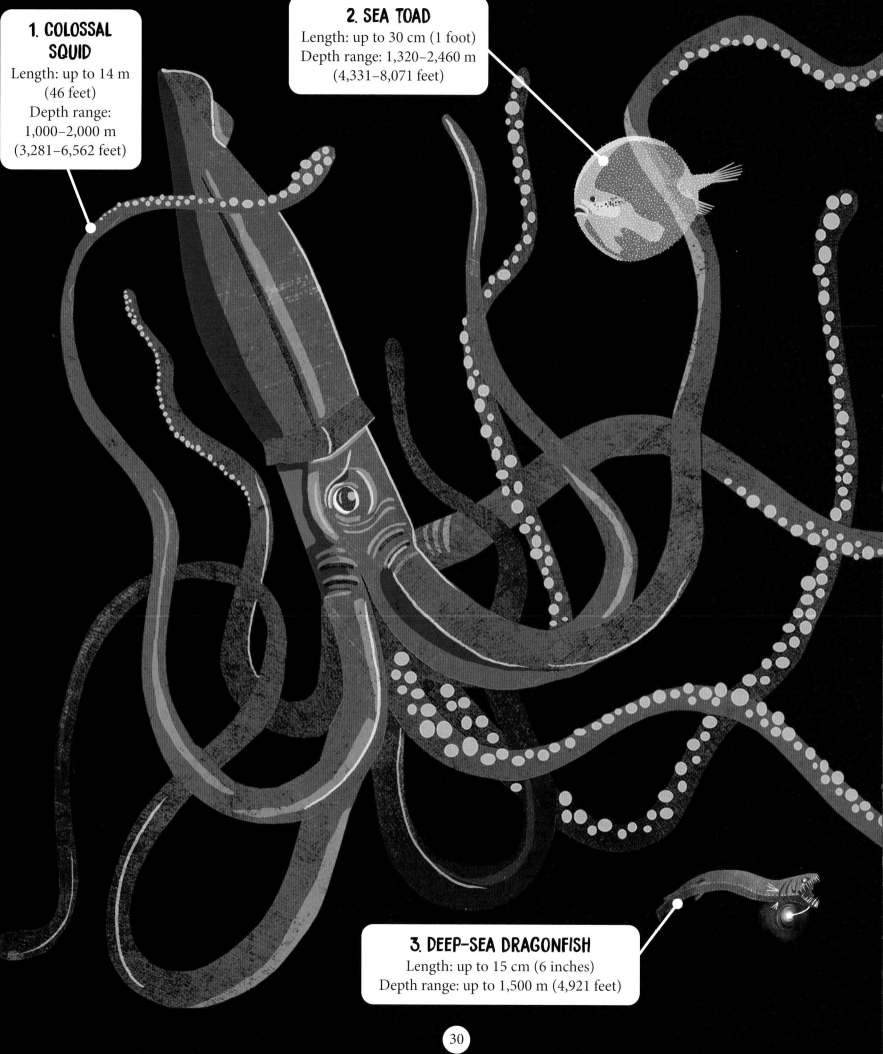

1. COLOSSAL SQUID
Length: up to 14 m (46 feet)
Depth range: 1,000–2,000 m (3,281–6,562 feet)

2. SEA TOAD
Length: up to 30 cm (1 foot)
Depth range: 1,320–2,460 m (4,331–8,071 feet)

3. DEEP-SEA DRAGONFISH
Length: up to 15 cm (6 inches)
Depth range: up to 1,500 m (4,921 feet)

4. COOKIECUTTER SHARK
Length: 42–56 cm (1.3–1.8 feet)
Depth range: 0–3,000 m (0–9,843 feet)

5. FRILLED SHARK
Length: up to 2 m (6.5 feet)
Depth range: 120–1,570 m (394–5,151 feet)

6. GULPER EEL
Length: 1–2 m (3–6.5 feet)
Depth range: 500–3,000 m
(1,640–9,843 feet)

PREDATORS OF THE MIDNIGHT ZONE

PREY IS SCARCE IN THE MIDNIGHT ZONE, AND PREDATORS HAVE DEVELOPED ADAPTATIONS TO SURVIVE THERE, INCLUDING LONG, SHARP, BACKWARD-POINTING TEETH TO ENSURE THAT PREY, ONCE CAUGHT, CAN'T WRIGGLE FREE. IN THE ABSOLUTE QUIET OF THE MIDNIGHT ZONE, MANY PREDATORS HAVE HIGHLY DEVELOPED HEARING. ONE FAMILY OF SNAKETOOTH FISHES 'LISTEN' WITH THEIR FACES.

1 COLOSSAL SQUID Colossal squid are superbly adapted to hunting in the dark depths. They have the largest eyes in the animal kingdom, and the biggest beaks of any squid. There are 25 rotating hooks on the ends of their tentacles for seizing prey.

2 SEA TOAD The sea toad saves energy by barely moving at all, breathing by pushing water across its gills. It sits on the seafloor and waits, motionless, for prey to come within reach. It doesn't need to feed often, and isn't picky about what it eats.

3 DEEP-SEA DRAGONFISH These fish have light organs next to their eyes that produce blue and red light. Emitting red light effectively makes them invisible to their prey. Dragonfish have large jaws and can eat prey more than half their own length.

4 COOKIECUTTER SHARK This little shark lures predators with bioluminescence, and attaches itself to them with its thick, sucking lips. Then, with its razor-sharp, hook-like teeth, it cuts out a plug of flesh, leaving a crater wound.

5 FRILLED SHARK The frilled shark hunts above the seabed, lunging at its prey like a snake. It has several rows of small, needle-sharp teeth ideal for snagging the soft bodies of squid, its favourite prey. Its long flexible jaws enable it to swallow prey whole.

6 GULPER EEL The gulper, or pelican eel, has an enormous scoop for a mouth, which it uses as a net as it swims into groups of small crustaceans. It then expels the water through its gills. Its tail has tentacles that glow pink to attract prey.

0 M (0 FEET)

1,000 M (3,281 FEET)

2,000 M (6,562 FEET)

3,000 M (9,843 FEET)

4,000 M (13,123 FEET)

5,000 M (16,404 FEET)

6,000 M (19,685 FEET)

7,000 M (22,966 FEET)

8,000 M (26,247 FEET)

9,000 M (29,528 FEET)

10,000 M (32,808 FEET)

11,000 M (36,089 FEET)

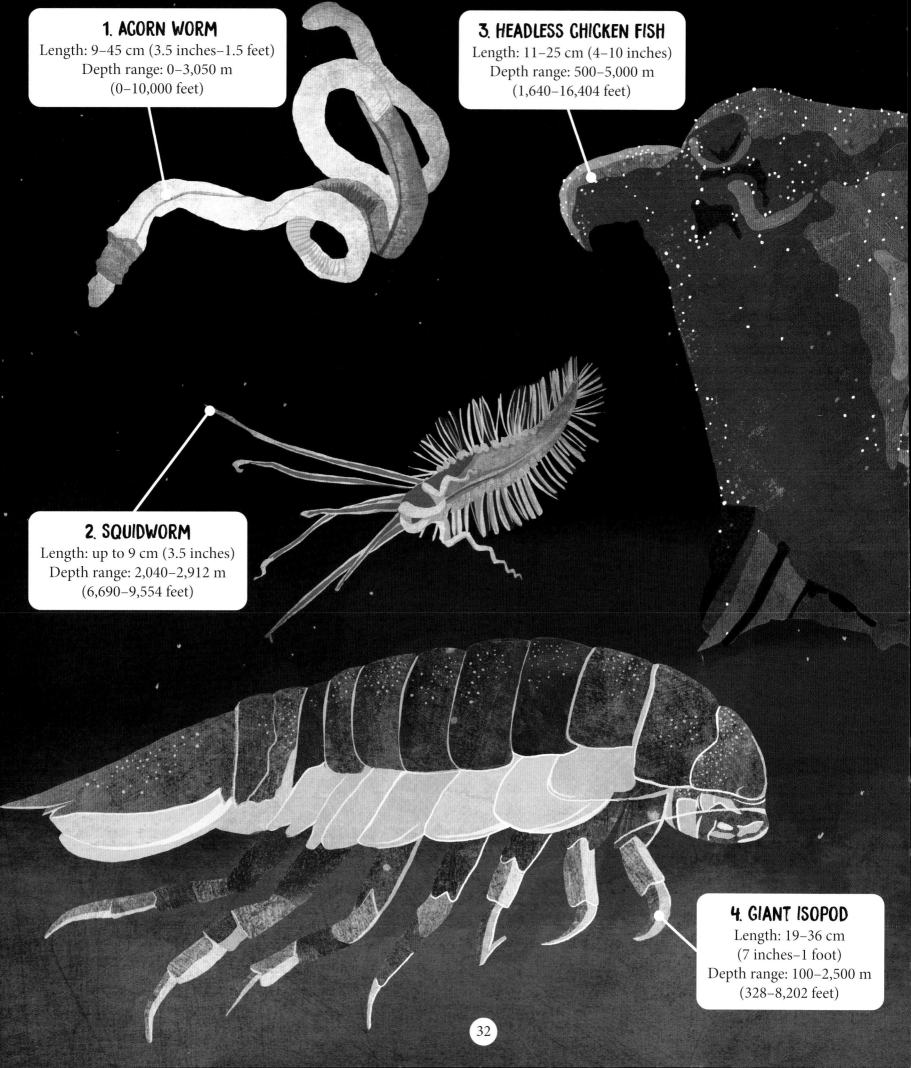

1. ACORN WORM
Length: 9–45 cm (3.5 inches–1.5 feet)
Depth range: 0–3,050 m
(0–10,000 feet)

3. HEADLESS CHICKEN FISH
Length: 11–25 cm (4–10 inches)
Depth range: 500–5,000 m
(1,640–16,404 feet)

2. SQUIDWORM
Length: up to 9 cm (3.5 inches)
Depth range: 2,040–2,912 m
(6,690–9,554 feet)

4. GIANT ISOPOD
Length: 19–36 cm
(7 inches–1 foot)
Depth range: 100–2,500 m
(328–8,202 feet)

5. ZOMBIE WORM
Length: 2–7 cm (0.7–3 inches)
Depth range: up to 4,000 m
(13,123 feet)

6. SQUAT LOBSTER
Length: up to 6.7 cm (3 inches)
Depth range: 12–1,463 m
(39–4,800 feet)

DEEP-SEA SCAVENGERS

IN THE MIDNIGHT ZONE, SCAVENGERS ARE EITHER OPEN-WATER DWELLERS, SUCH AS THE AMPHIPOD, CONSUMING MARINE SNOW AS IT FALLS, OR BOTTOM-DWELLERS, LIKE THE SLIMESTAR, SIFTING THROUGH THE SILT ON THE OCEAN FLOOR FOR ORGANIC MATTER. AN IMPORTANT SOURCE OF NUTRITION IS WHALE FALL – WHALE CARCASSES THAT FALL TO THE OCEAN FLOOR.

1 ACORN WORM Acorn worms live in burrows on the seafloor. Some eat by swallowing sand or mud that contains organic matter. Others collect particles from the water. A third species moves across the seabed, sucking up detritus and excreting a trail of waste.

2 SQUIDWORM The squidworm is a worm with ten tentacles on its head, making it look a bit like a squid – eight are used for breathing and the other two are for collecting food in the form of particles of marine snow (see page 28) falling from above.

3 HEADLESS CHICKEN FISH This unusual-looking sea cucumber spends most of its time swimming, landing only briefly on the seafloor to feed. Its webbed fins allow it to journey up to 1,000 m (3,281 feet) to find new feeding grounds and avoid predators.

4 GIANT ISOPOD These crustaceans look like huge woodlice. They spend most of their time on the seabed waiting for food to fall from higher up. Their very slow metabolisms allow them to wait sometimes years without eating.

5 ZOMBIE WORM These worms eat the bones of dead whales on the seafloor. Lacking a mouth and stomach, they don't eat the bone directly. Their skin secretes an acid that dissolves the bone into fat and protein, which is eaten by bacteria that are living inside the worm.

6 SQUAT LOBSTER Squat lobsters lack a shell, and hide in crevices to protect themselves from predators. From here, they reach out with their long arms and sift through the sand for sunken food. Sometimes they steal food from sea anemones.

0 M (0 FEET)
1,000 M (3,281 FEET)
2,000 M (6,562 FEET)
3,000 M (9,843 FEET)
4,000 M (13,123 FEET)
5,000 M (16,404 FEET)
6,000 M (19,685 FEET)
7,000 M (22,966 FEET)
8,000 M (26,247 FEET)
9,000 M (29,528 FEET)
10,000 M (32,808 FEET)
11,000 M (36,089 FEET)

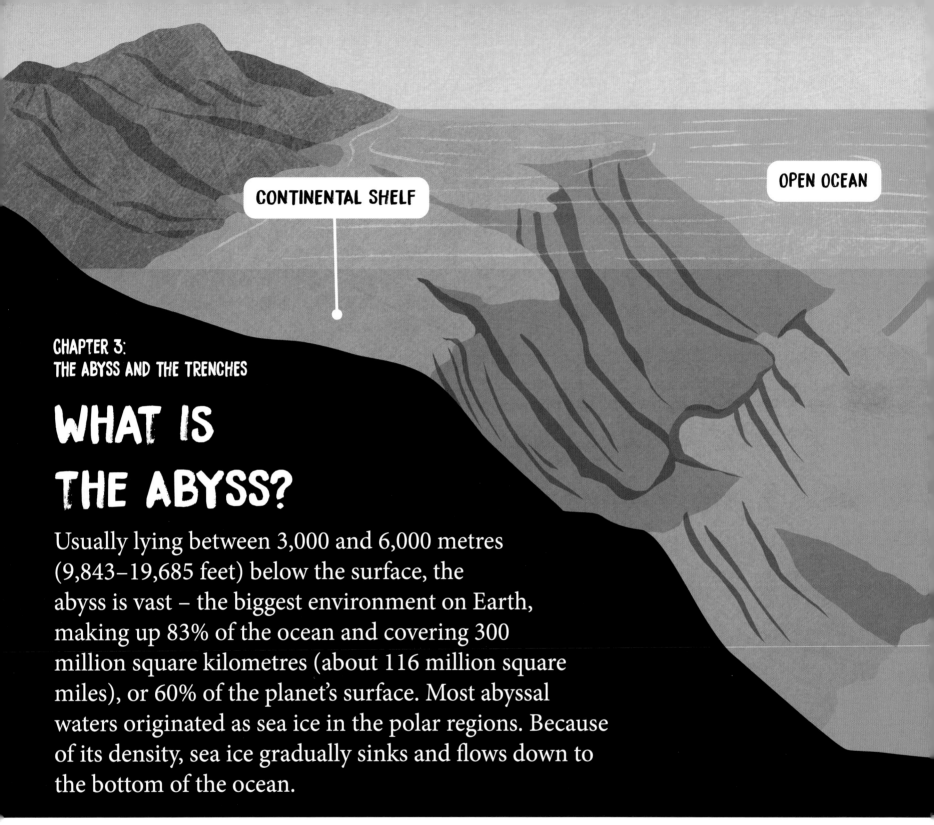

CONTINENTAL SHELF

OPEN OCEAN

CHAPTER 3:
THE ABYSS AND THE TRENCHES

WHAT IS THE ABYSS?

Usually lying between 3,000 and 6,000 metres (9,843–19,685 feet) below the surface, the abyss is vast – the biggest environment on Earth, making up 83% of the ocean and covering 300 million square kilometres (about 116 million square miles), or 60% of the planet's surface. Most abyssal waters originated as sea ice in the polar regions. Because of its density, sea ice gradually sinks and flows down to the bottom of the ocean.

CREATURES OF THE ABYSS

The abyss contains a range of animals, including crustaceans, molluscs (such as snails and squid) and fish. The majority of these creatures live on the seafloor or less than 5 metres (16 feet) above it, where most of the nutrients can be found. To cope with the lack of food, these animals have a very slow metabolism. They move very slowly and reproduce quite rarely to conserve energy. Some animals attached to the seabed have stalks to rise above the water at the bottom, where oxygen is scarce. There are no sharks or rays in the abyss, but some visit from the midnight zone in order to hunt.

CRUSTACEANS

Crustaceans are a family of invertebrates that include crabs, lobsters and shrimps. One common deep-sea crustacean is the amphipod.

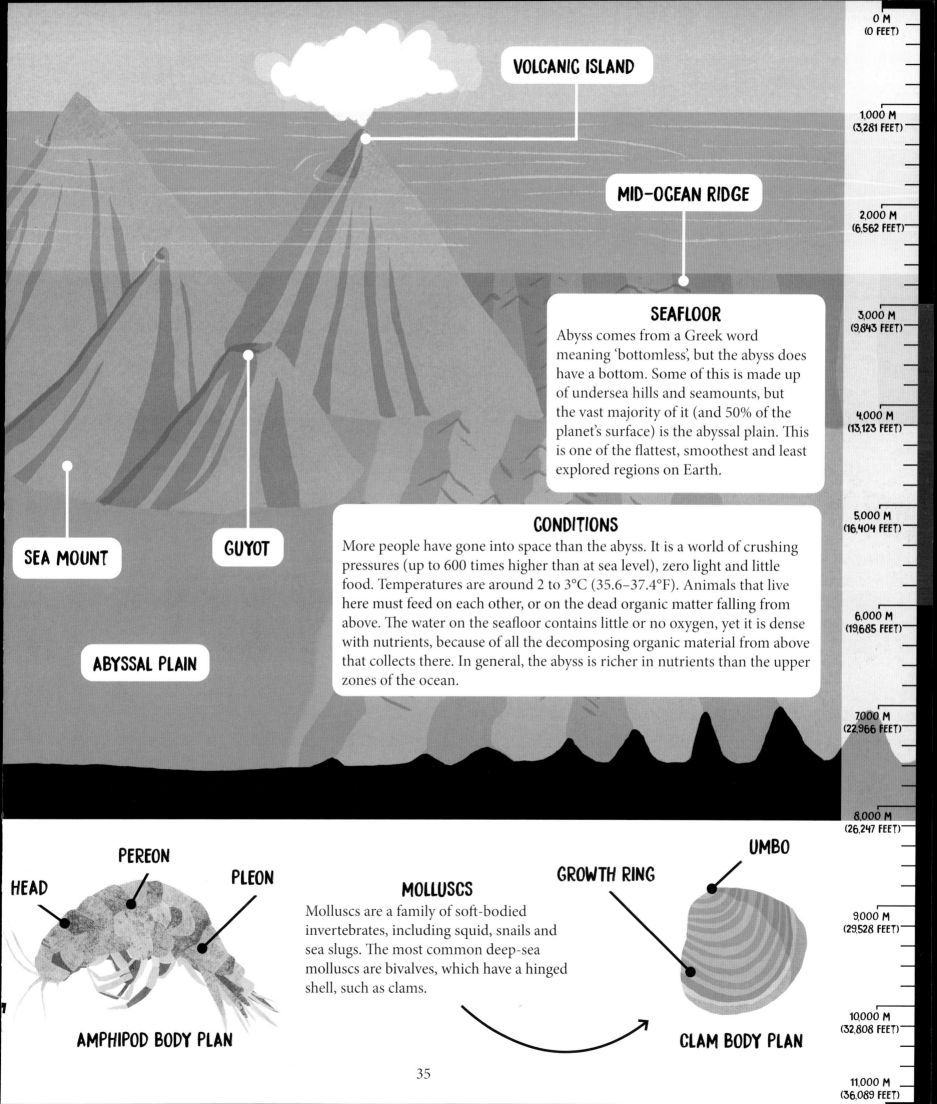

VOLCANIC ISLAND

MID-OCEAN RIDGE

0 M
(0 FEET)

1,000 M
(3,281 FEET)

2,000 M
(6,562 FEET)

SEAFLOOR

Abyss comes from a Greek word meaning 'bottomless', but the abyss does have a bottom. Some of this is made up of undersea hills and seamounts, but the vast majority of it (and 50% of the planet's surface) is the abyssal plain. This is one of the flattest, smoothest and least explored regions on Earth.

3,000 M
(9,843 FEET)

4,000 M
(13,123 FEET)

CONDITIONS

More people have gone into space than the abyss. It is a world of crushing pressures (up to 600 times higher than at sea level), zero light and little food. Temperatures are around 2 to 3°C (35.6–37.4°F). Animals that live here must feed on each other, or on the dead organic matter falling from above. The water on the seafloor contains little or no oxygen, yet it is dense with nutrients, because of all the decomposing organic material from above that collects there. In general, the abyss is richer in nutrients than the upper zones of the ocean.

5,000 M
(16,404 FEET)

6,000 M
(19,685 FEET)

SEA MOUNT

GUYOT

ABYSSAL PLAIN

7,000 M
(22,966 FEET)

8,000 M
(26,247 FEET)

PEREON

PLEON

HEAD

UMBO

GROWTH RING

MOLLUSCS

Molluscs are a family of soft-bodied invertebrates, including squid, snails and sea slugs. The most common deep-sea molluscs are bivalves, which have a hinged shell, such as clams.

9,000 M
(29,528 FEET)

AMPHIPOD BODY PLAN

CLAM BODY PLAN

10,000 M
(32,808 FEET)

11,000 M
(36,089 FEET)

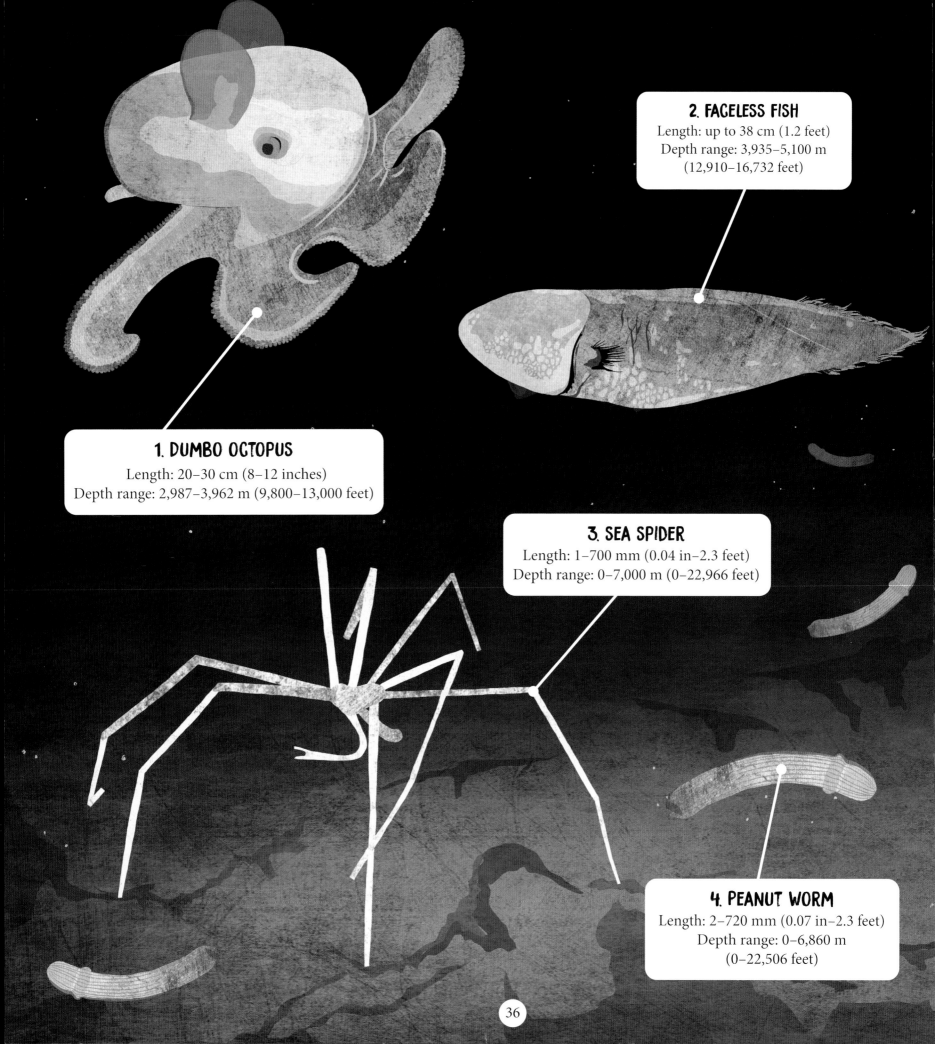

2. FACELESS FISH
Length: up to 38 cm (1.2 feet)
Depth range: 3,935–5,100 m
(12,910–16,732 feet)

1. DUMBO OCTOPUS
Length: 20–30 cm (8–12 inches)
Depth range: 2,987–3,962 m (9,800–13,000 feet)

3. SEA SPIDER
Length: 1–700 mm (0.04 in–2.3 feet)
Depth range: 0–7,000 m (0–22,966 feet)

4. PEANUT WORM
Length: 2–720 mm (0.07 in–2.3 feet)
Depth range: 0–6,860 m
(0–22,506 feet)

5. SEA CUCUMBER
Average length: 10–30 cm
(4–12 inches)
Depth range: 0–10,687 m
(0–35,062 feet)

6. TRIPOD FISH
Average length: up to 30 cm (1 foot)
Depth range: 900–4,700 m (2,953–15,420 feet)

AMAZING ANIMALS OF THE ABYSS

THE CREATURES THAT DWELL IN THESE DEPTHS HAVE DEVELOPED EXTRAORDINARY ADAPTATIONS TO SURVIVE. THEY TEND TO BE SMALL BUT HAVE LARGE, FLEXIBLE STOMACHS AND BIG MOUTHS SO THEY CAN SWALLOW AS MUCH FOOD AS POSSIBLE ON THE RARE OCCASIONS THEY FIND ANY. SCIENTISTS BELIEVE THAT MORE THAN 90% OF ABYSSAL ANIMALS USE BIOLUMINESCENCE TO LURE OR FIND PREY OR FIND MATES.

1 DUMBO OCTOPUS The arms of the dumbo octopus are connected by a web of skin, making them look like umbrellas when their arms are spread. They move slowly by flapping their ear-like fins, hunting for invertebrates living just above the sea floor.

2 FACELESS FISH The mouth of this strange fish is underneath its body, and its eyes are buried deep beneath its skin, making it look like it doesn't have a face. Scientists believe it uses sensory organs in its jelly-like head to navigate and find prey.

3 SEA SPIDER Sea spiders live deep in the ocean around Antarctica and can grow to enormous sizes. They have no body, just eight legs that carry their vital organs, and a long, tubular mouthpart that sucks up their prey. They breathe through holes in their legs.

4 PEANUT WORM The peanut worm's body is made up of a bulging trunk and a narrower front part called the introvert. It feeds by extending the introvert to gather food particles and draw them into its mouth. If threatened, it can retract the introvert and shrink into a ball.

5 SEA CUCUMBER These are soft-bodied creatures that live on or near the ocean floor, sometimes partially buried in it. They use tentacle-like tube feet to move around and to feed. Their diet consists of plankton and tiny particles of decaying organic matter.

6 TRIPOD FISH This fish has three fins up to a metre (3 feet) long, which it uses for standing on the seafloor. They place it at a height to catch any passing crustacean. The fish senses its prey with its front fins.

0 M
(0 FEET)

1,000 M
(3,281 FEET)

2,000 M
(6,562 FEET)

3,000 M
(9,843 FEET)

4,000 M
(13,123 FEET)

5,000 M
(16,404 FEET)

6,000 M
(19,685 FEET)

7,000 M
(22,966 FEET)

8,000 M
(26,247 FEET)

9,000 M
(29,528 FEET)

10,000 M
(32,808 FEET)

11,000 M
(36,089 FEET)

3. ZOARCID FISH
Length: up to 61 cm (2 feet)
Depth range: below 2,300 m (7,546 feet)

2. VULCAN OCTOPUS
Length: up to 18.4 cm
(7.2 inches)
Depth range: below 2,200 m
(7,218 feet)

1. KIWA CRAB
Length: up to 15 cm (6 inches)
Depth range: below 2,200 m
(7,218 feet)

4. SCALY-FOOT SNAIL
Length: up to 1.5 cm (0.6 inch)
Depth range: 2,400–2,900 m
(7,874–9,514 feet)

5. GIANT VENT MUSSEL
Length: up to 40 cm (1.3 feet)
Depth range: below 2,800 m
(9,186 feet)

6. GIANT TUBE WORM
Length: up to 3 m (10 feet)
Depth range: below 1,600 m
(5,249 feet)

HYDROTHERMAL VENTS

HYDROTHERMAL VENTS ARE OPENINGS ON THE OCEAN FLOOR FOUND AT DEPTHS OF 1,600–7,700 M (5,249–25,262 FEET). SUPER-HOT, MINERAL-RICH WATER SPEWS FROM THESE VENTS. BACTERIA CONVERT CHEMICALS FROM THE VENT INTO NUTRIENTS, CREATING AN ENVIRONMENT THAT CAN SUPPORT A DIVERSE COMMUNITY OF ANIMALS.

1 KIWA CRAB This crustacean, also known as the yeti crab for its hairy pincers, feeds off the bacteria growing on these hairs. It encourages the bacteria to grow by waving its pincers through the waters around the vent, and then scrapes them off and eats them.

2 VULCAN OCTOPUS The vulcan octopus feeds on small crustaceans living around the hydrothermal vents. Adapted for the dark of the deep ocean, it uses touch and smell, not vision. Its two front arms are longer and used for feeling its way and hunting, while the rear arms are used for moving around.

3 ZOARCID FISH Zoarcids, or pink vent fish, are top predators in the vent community. They eat tubeworms, shrimps, limpets and snails. By eating limpets attached to rocks, they help other organisms to settle there, improving biodiversity.

4 SCALY-FOOT SNAIL The bacteria living within the scaly-foot snail help build it an armour-plated shell made of iron sulphide, giving it a powerful defence against predators. No other animal on earth is able to use iron in this way.

5 GIANT VENT MUSSEL These huge mussels have bacteria living in their gills that consume sulphides and methane from the hydrothermal vent and convert them into organic carbon that the mussel can use for energy and food.

6 GIANT TUBE WORM Giant tube worms are free-swimming as larvae, but then attach themselves to rocks. They have no mouth or digestive tract. The bacteria living inside them convert chemicals from the hydrothermal vent into food for them to live on.

0 M (0 FEET)

1,000 M (3,281 FEET)

2,000 M (6,562 FEET)

3,000 M (9,843 FEET)

4,000 M (13,123 FEET)

5,000 M (16,404 FEET)

6,000 M (19,685 FEET)

7,000 M (22,966 FEET)

8,000 M (26,247 FEET)

9,000 M (29,528 FEET)

10,000 M (32,808 FEET)

11,000 M (36,089 FEET)

Like hydrothermal vents, cold seeps are cracks in the ocean floor caused by movements of the Earth's crust. These are found at all depths, but especially in the Hadal zone. The deepest yet found is in the Japan Trench at a depth of 7,326 m (24,035 feet). Hydrogen sulphide, methane and other chemicals leak out of these cracks. They are not super-hot like hydrothermal vents, but they provide an environment for life in a similar way: bacteria obtain energy from the chemicals and convert them into organic nutrients that support a community of animals.

WHAT ARE THE TRENCHES?

Beneath the abyss there exists yet another zone – the deepest of all the ocean habitats. Scientists call it the Hadal zone, named after the underworld Hades in Greek mythology. It is made up of a series of V-shaped chasms called trenches and deep basins called troughs. They span depths of 6,000 to nearly 11,000 metres (19,685–36,089 feet). There are 46 hadal habitats worldwide, comprised of 33 trenches and 13 troughs. Most of them are found in the Pacific Ocean. Temperatures in the Hadal zone range from 1–4°C (33.8–39.2°F).

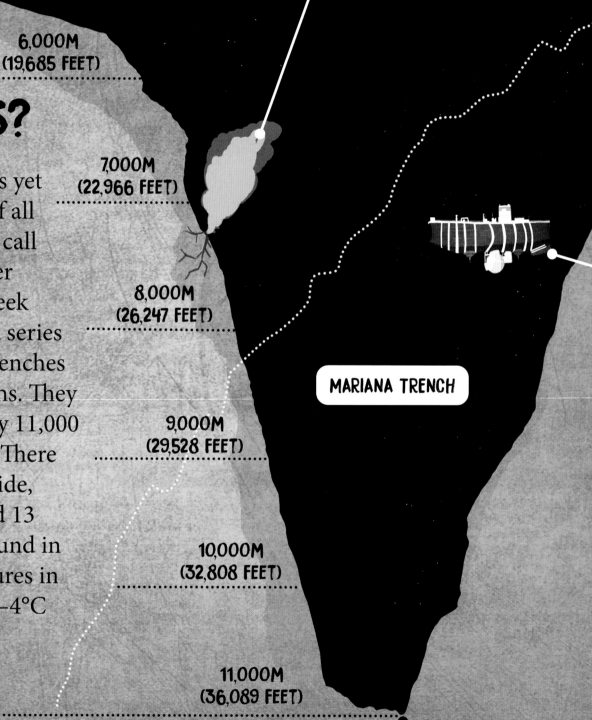

6,000M
(19,685 FEET)

7,000M
(22,966 FEET)

8,000M
(26,247 FEET)

9,000M
(29,528 FEET)

MARIANA TRENCH

10,000M
(32,808 FEET)

11,000M
(36,089 FEET)

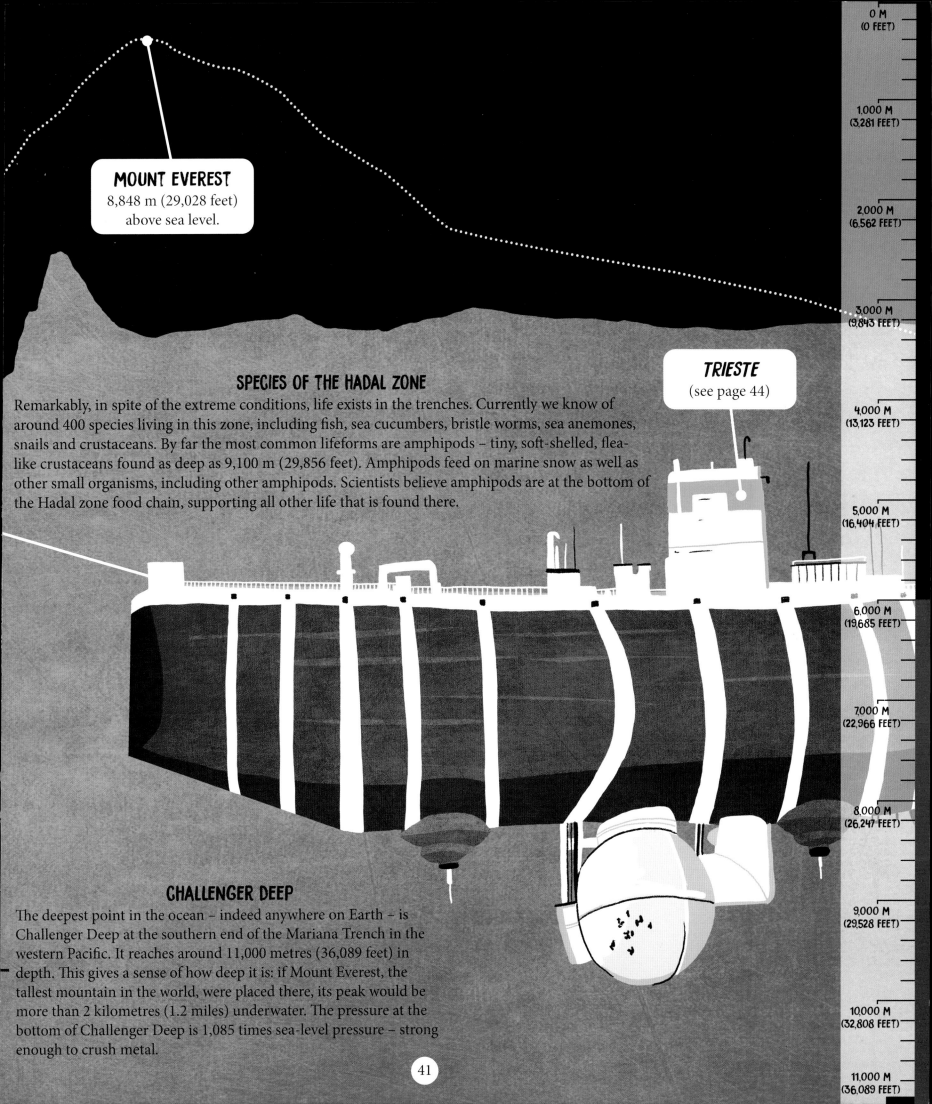

MOUNT EVEREST
8,848 m (29,028 feet)
above sea level.

1,000 M
(3,281 FEET)

2,000 M
(6,562 FEET)

3,000 M
(9,843 FEET)

TRIESTE
(see page 44)

4,000 M
(13,123 FEET)

SPECIES OF THE HADAL ZONE

Remarkably, in spite of the extreme conditions, life exists in the trenches. Currently we know of around 400 species living in this zone, including fish, sea cucumbers, bristle worms, sea anemones, snails and crustaceans. By far the most common lifeforms are amphipods – tiny, soft-shelled, flea-like crustaceans found as deep as 9,100 m (29,856 feet). Amphipods feed on marine snow as well as other small organisms, including other amphipods. Scientists believe amphipods are at the bottom of the Hadal zone food chain, supporting all other life that is found there.

5,000 M
(16,404 FEET)

6,000 M
(19,685 FEET)

7,000 M
(22,966 FEET)

8,000 M
(26,247 FEET)

CHALLENGER DEEP

The deepest point in the ocean – indeed anywhere on Earth – is Challenger Deep at the southern end of the Mariana Trench in the western Pacific. It reaches around 11,000 metres (36,089 feet) in depth. This gives a sense of how deep it is: if Mount Everest, the tallest mountain in the world, were placed there, its peak would be more than 2 kilometres (1.2 miles) underwater. The pressure at the bottom of Challenger Deep is 1,085 times sea-level pressure – strong enough to crush metal.

9,000 M
(29,528 FEET)

10,000 M
(32,808 FEET)

41

11,000 M
(36,089 FEET)

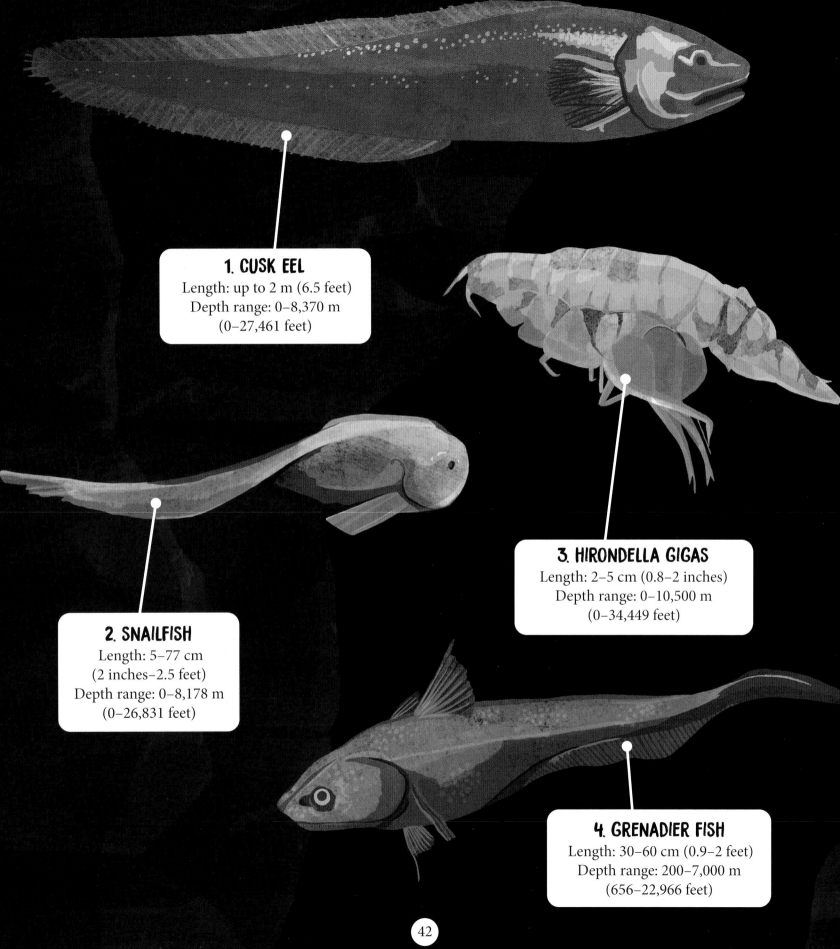

1. CUSK EEL
Length: up to 2 m (6.5 feet)
Depth range: 0–8,370 m
(0–27,461 feet)

2. SNAILFISH
Length: 5–77 cm
(2 inches–2.5 feet)
Depth range: 0–8,178 m
(0–26,831 feet)

3. HIRONDELLA GIGAS
Length: 2–5 cm (0.8–2 inches)
Depth range: 0–10,500 m
(0–34,449 feet)

4. GRENADIER FISH
Length: 30–60 cm (0.9–2 feet)
Depth range: 200–7,000 m
(656–22,966 feet)

5. SUPERGIANT AMPHIPOD
Length: up to 34 cm (1.1 feet)
Depth range: 6,000 m (19,685 feet)

6. BENTHESICYMUS PRAWN
Length: 20–30 cm (8–12 inches)
Depth range: up to 7,703 m
(25,272 feet)

LIFE IN THE TRENCHES

HADAL ANIMALS OFTEN LACK EYES AND HAVE EVOLVED SENSES THAT CAN DETECT MOVEMENTS IN THE WATER. MOST ARE SCAVENGERS, FEEDING OFF ORGANIC MATTER ON THE TRENCH FLOOR. FISH TEND TO HAVE TRANSPARENT, GELATINOUS FLESH, WITH SKELETONS OF CARTILAGE RATHER THAN BONE TO HELP THEM SURVIVE THE EXTRAORDINARY PRESSURES. THE DEEPEST FISH EVER DISCOVERED WAS A CUSK EEL FOUND AT 8,370 M (27,461 FEET).

1 CUSK EEL These blind, eel-like fish hunt amphipods and plankton using sensory pores on their head that detect vibrations. They can withstand the pressures thanks to a jelly-like layer of tissue beneath their skin and a skeleton strengthened with extra bone material.

2 SNAILFISH The dominant fish of the Hadal zone, they have gelatinous, tadpole-shaped bodies, a skeleton of cartilage, and translucent skin revealing their inner organs. To survive the high pressures, they produce a substance that keeps their cells from collapsing.

3 HIRONDELLA GIGAS These amphipods survive by scavenging particles of wood from trees that get swept into the ocean and then sink to the bottom. Unsurprisingly for animals with such a particular diet, they are able to survive a long time between meals.

4 GRENADIER FISH Hadal-zone grenadiers have evolved a sensory organ called a lateral line to sense movement in the surrounding water. They are bottom feeders, often found around cold seeps.

5 SUPERGIANT AMPHIPOD These scary-looking crustaceans are more than 20 times larger than the typical amphipod. They only live at extreme depths, on the abyssal plain and in the trenches.

6 BENTHESICYMUS PRAWN This crustacean is a decapod, related to shrimps and crabs. Until it was discovered living in the Kermadec and Mariana trenches in 2009, scientists believed decapods could not survive in the Hadal zone. It preys on small amphipods for food.

0 M (0 FEET)
1,000 M (3,281 FEET)
2,000 M (6,562 FEET)
3,000 M (9,843 FEET)
4,000 M (13,123 FEET)
5,000 M (16,404 FEET)
6,000 M (19,685 FEET)
7,000 M (22,966 FEET)
8,000 M (26,247 FEET)
9,000 M (29,528 FEET)
10,000 M (32,808 FEET)
11,000 M (36,089 FEET)

EXPLORING THE OCEAN DEPTHS TODAY

For most of human history, the deep ocean has been a realm of mystery. It's only in the last century that we've begun to develop technologies that allow us to penetrate this alien world far beneath the waves. The deepest dive by a human using SCUBA equipment is just over 300 metres (984 feet) – a little way into the twilight zone. Systematic exploration of the deep ocean can only be done using underwater craft – submersibles.

PILOTED SUBMERSIBLES

Exploration with submersibles began in the 1930s with ball-shaped vehicles called bathyspheres lowered by cables from a ship. These couldn't move around or collect samples. Later, bathyscaphs ('deep boats') were developed that had some ability to manoeuvre. The most famous of these was *Trieste*, which took its two occupants to Challenger Deep, the deepest point on Earth, in 1960. Four years later, the deep-ocean research submersible, *Alvin*, was built. *Alvin* can carry three people and has made more than 5,000 dives for the study of the landscape and lifeforms of the deep ocean.

SCUBA DIVER

AUV

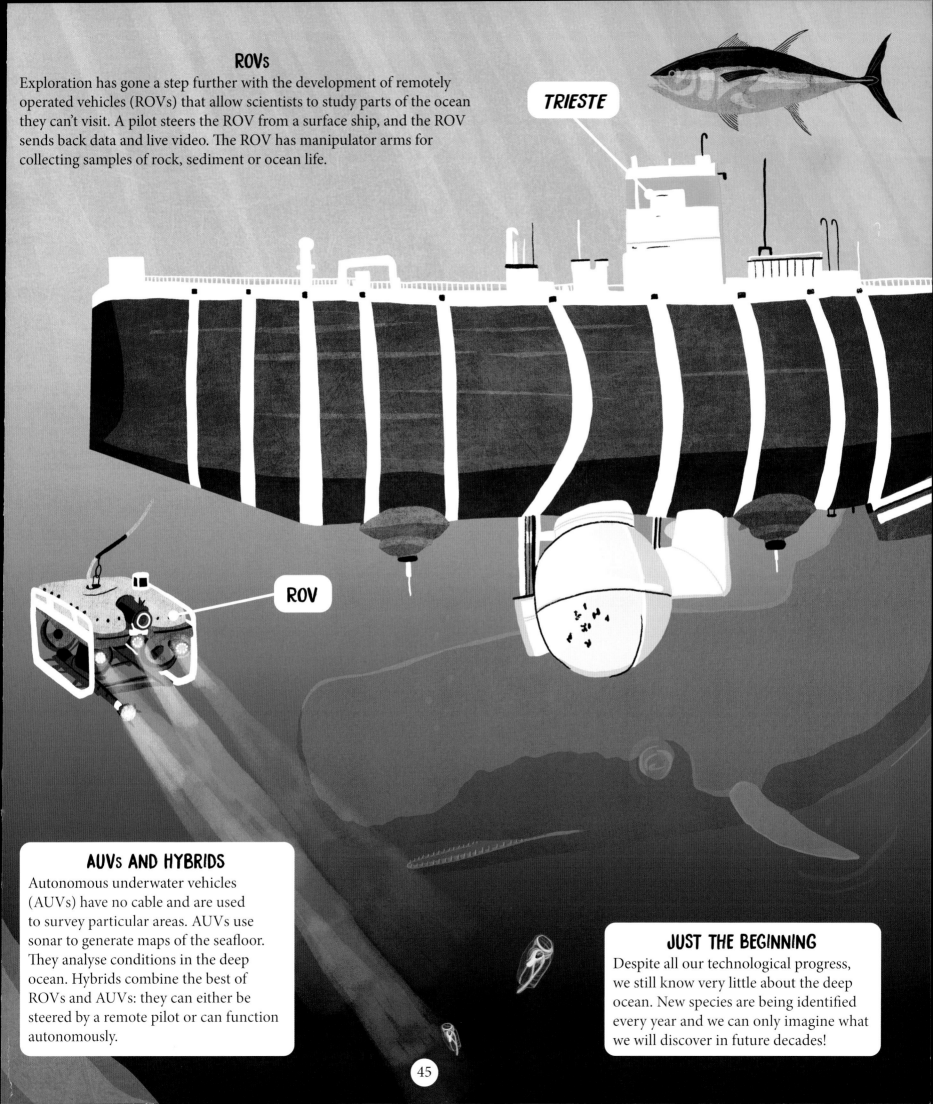

ROVs

Exploration has gone a step further with the development of remotely operated vehicles (ROVs) that allow scientists to study parts of the ocean they can't visit. A pilot steers the ROV from a surface ship, and the ROV sends back data and live video. The ROV has manipulator arms for collecting samples of rock, sediment or ocean life.

TRIESTE

ROV

AUVs AND HYBRIDS

Autonomous underwater vehicles (AUVs) have no cable and are used to survey particular areas. AUVs use sonar to generate maps of the seafloor. They analyse conditions in the deep ocean. Hybrids combine the best of ROVs and AUVs: they can either be steered by a remote pilot or can function autonomously.

JUST THE BEGINNING

Despite all our technological progress, we still know very little about the deep ocean. New species are being identified every year and we can only imagine what we will discover in future decades!

CLIMATE CHANGE

Since the Industrial Revolution, the amount of carbon dioxide (CO_2) in the atmosphere has increased by over 35%, primarily due to the burning of fossil fuels. The extra CO_2 traps more of the Sun's heat in the atmosphere, causing a rise in average global temperatures and changing weather systems. This is known as climate change.

THE ARCTIC OCEAN

The Arctic Ocean is warming at twice the rate of the global average, threatening the wildlife living there. Polar bears, for example, rely on sea ice as a platform from which to hunt. With sea ice melting earlier each spring and forming later in the autumn, the bears have to go longer without eating, causing many of them, and their cubs, to starve.

CHANGING MIGRATION PATTERNS

Each winter, blacktip sharks migrate south to the coast of Florida, USA, where they help preserve the ecosystems of coral reefs and seagrass beds by eating weak and sick fish. With rising ocean temperatures, many of these sharks now remain in cooler, northern waters and no longer play this vital role. Similar changes in migration patterns have been observed among right whales, salmon, mackerel, Atlantic cod and many other species. Marine life in general is shifting towards the cooler polar regions. This disrupts complex food webs and the patterns of ocean life.

ALGAL BLOOMS

Warming temperatures have also led to destructive algal blooms (a rapid increase in the population of algae), which reduce the oxygen content of parts of the ocean, creating lifeless 'marine deserts'. Algal blooms damage coral reefs, seagrasses and kelp forests and harm the animals that live in these habitats by lowering the oxygen levels in the water.

ACIDIFICATION

The ocean plays a major role in reducing the effects of climate change. Over the past 200 years the ocean has absorbed one-third of the CO_2 and 90% of the extra heat produced by human activities. At the same time, the ocean is being damaged by climate change. The continual absorption of CO_2 has increased the acidity of the oceans by 30% over the past two centuries. When combined with warming temperatures, it can cause the destruction of coral reefs – an effect known as coral bleaching – with devastating consequences for the species that live there.

RISING SEA LEVELS

One of the major impacts of climate change has been rising sea levels. Average sea levels have risen by around 23 cm (9 inches) since 1880. Every year, the sea rises by another 3.2 mm (0.1 inches), and the rate is increasing. Some scientists estimate that in the next 90 years, the seas could rise by 1 metre (3.2 feet). This is a major threat to offshore and coastal habitats and the people and animals that live there.

CAUSES

There are three main reasons for this change in sea levels. Firstly, when water gets warmer, it expands. Secondly, global warming is causing the ice sheets that cover Greenland and Antarctica to melt at a faster rate, and more of this meltwater runs into the ocean. Thirdly, mountain glaciers (dense bodies of ice) are also melting more than they used to during the summer months, sending yet more meltwater into the ocean via rivers and streams.

OFFSHORE HABITATS

Many of the environments we have looked at in this book, such as coral reefs, seagrass meadows and kelp beds, depend on stable sea levels. As shallow seas get deeper, the amount of sunlight reaching seagrass, kelp and the algae living in coral, which depend on photosynthesis, will be reduced. Sea level rises also increase coastal erosion, washing sediment into the sea and further reducing the sunlight coming through the water.

BEACH HABITATS

Sea turtles make their nests in beach sand, and many species return to the same beaches where they hatched to lay the eggs for the next generation. Sea level rises could erode beaches and flood turtle nests. The loss of beaches will also affect other species such as shorebirds, sand crabs and beach hoppers.

COASTAL WETLANDS

Rising sea levels will flood coastal wetlands such as mangrove forests and salt marshes. Some scientists predict that mangrove forests, which grow in the coastal intertidal zones of warmer regions, could be wiped out by the year 2100. As well as providing a habitat for countless plants and animals, coastal wetlands provide a buffer against floods and storm surges that threaten coastal communities.

STORM SURGE

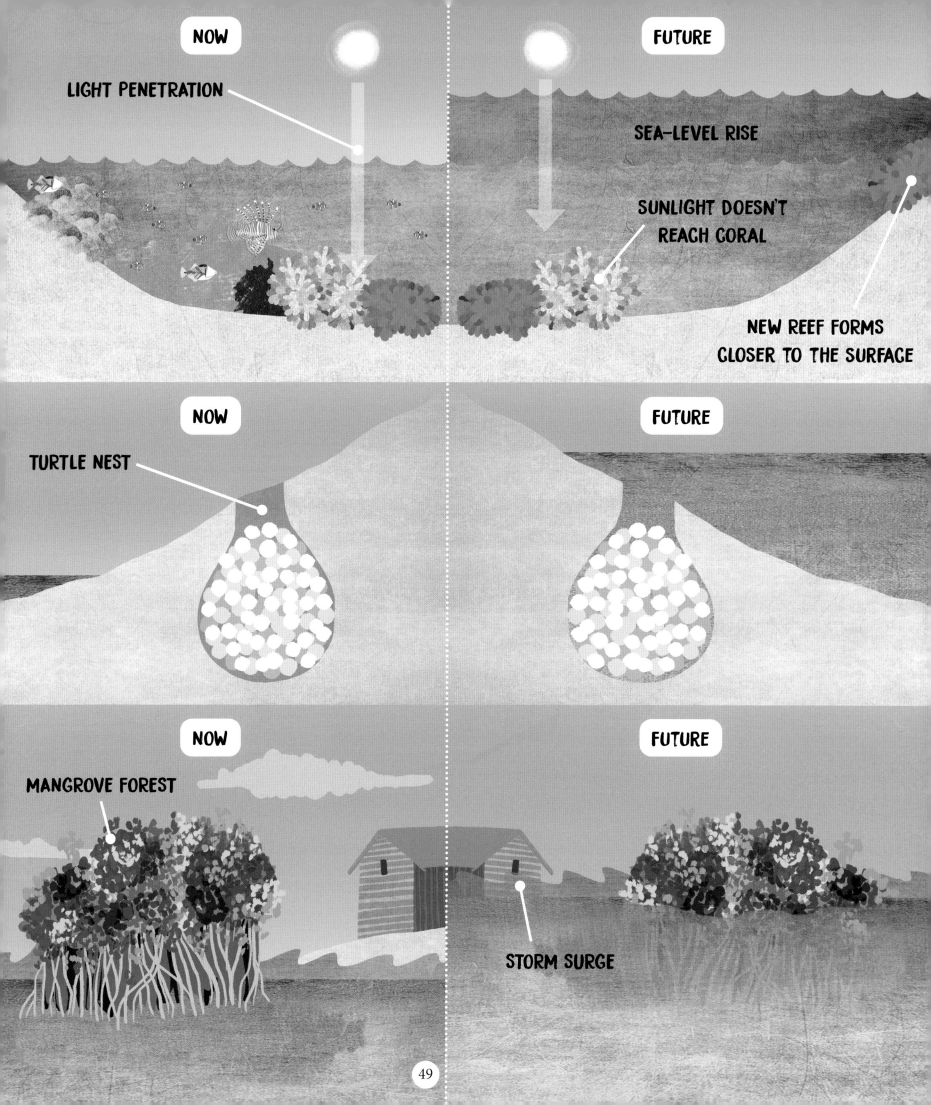

POLLUTION

Human activity produces vast amounts of waste every year, and much of this goes directly or indirectly into the ocean. Even the waste we produce inland often gets swept into the ocean via storm drains, sewers, rivers and streams. Pollution includes everyday litter, sewage, industrial waste and oil spills.

CHEMICAL POLLUTION

Chemical waste from farms and factories runs off the land into waterways that ultimately flow into the ocean. Many of these chemicals, especially nitrogen and phosphorus used in agricultural fertilisers, aid the growth of algal blooms. These create toxins, block sunlight, clog fish gills and lead to dead zones in the ocean where nothing can live or grow.

PLASTIC

Eighty percent of the litter that ends up in the ocean comes from the land. Most of this is plastic – shopping bags, water bottles, yoghurt pots, drinking straws etc. It is estimated that between 1.15 and 2.41 million tonnes of plastic enters the ocean each year. This is particularly bad news as plastic can take up to a thousand years to biodegrade and is a serious menace to marine life. Animals can get entangled in it or die from eating it. Small organisms such as plankton feed on particles of broken-down plastic called microplastic and absorb the chemicals from this into their tissues. When they are eaten by larger animals, they absorb the same chemicals into their tissues, and so on up the food chain.

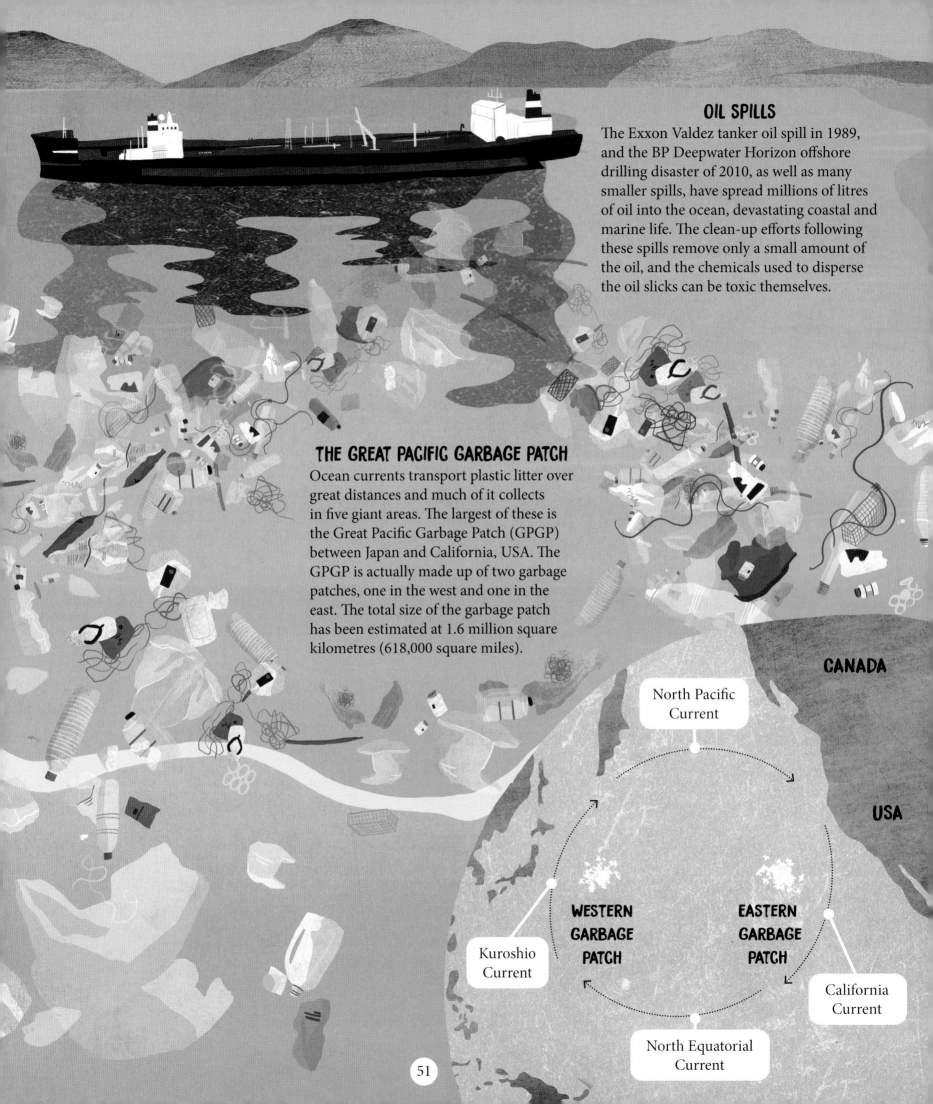

OIL SPILLS
The Exxon Valdez tanker oil spill in 1989, and the BP Deepwater Horizon offshore drilling disaster of 2010, as well as many smaller spills, have spread millions of litres of oil into the ocean, devastating coastal and marine life. The clean-up efforts following these spills remove only a small amount of the oil, and the chemicals used to disperse the oil slicks can be toxic themselves.

THE GREAT PACIFIC GARBAGE PATCH
Ocean currents transport plastic litter over great distances and much of it collects in five giant areas. The largest of these is the Great Pacific Garbage Patch (GPGP) between Japan and California, USA. The GPGP is actually made up of two garbage patches, one in the west and one in the east. The total size of the garbage patch has been estimated at 1.6 million square kilometres (618,000 square miles).

CANADA

USA

North Pacific Current

Kuroshio Current

WESTERN GARBAGE PATCH

EASTERN GARBAGE PATCH

California Current

North Equatorial Current

USE ENERGY-SAVING LIGHTBULBS.

WALK, CYCLE OR USE PUBLIC TRANSPORT.

TURN OFF APPLIANCES AFTER USE.

WEAR A JACKET WHEN COLD –
DON'T TURN YOUR HEATING ON.

WHAT CAN WE DO ABOUT IT?

There are many actions we can take in our everyday lives to help protect our oceans. We can do our bit to lower CO_2 emissions by saving energy – switching to compact fluorescent lightbulbs; riding a bike, walking or using public transport instead of a car; turning off appliances when not in use; and wearing a jumper instead of turning up the thermostat when it's cold.

REDUCE PLASTIC

To reduce plastic waste that may end up in the ocean, avoid single-use plastic items like drinking straws and drinks containers. Carry a reusable water bottle, use cloth grocery bags and store food in reusable containers.

PROTECT THE BEACH

When you visit the beach, always clean up afterwards so none of your litter ends up in the sea. Bring a bag with you for picking up trash. You could even go further and volunteer for local beach clean-ups.

BE CAREFUL WHAT YOU BUY

Fish stocks are declining around the world because of loss of habitat and overfishing. Talk to your family about the fish and seafood you buy. Choose items labelled 'line caught', 'diver caught', 'sustainably caught' or 'sustainably harvested'. You could think about cutting down on eating fish and eating more plant-based foods instead.

GIVE YOUR SUPPORT

There are many organisations that are working to protect ocean habitats and wildlife. Why not become a member and volunteer for some hands-on work or to help spread the word? Contact local politicians and find out what they are doing for ocean conservation. Ask your family to support local restaurants and food stores that only stock sustainable seafood.

NEVER STOP LEARNING

All life on Earth is connected to the ocean, and it's vital that we educate ourselves about this mysterious and beautiful realm. The more we learn, the more we will want to protect it. So when you discover something new and amazing about the ocean, share that knowledge and inspire others.

EXPLORING

Enjoy exploring nature, but try not to disturb the wildlife, and don't remove rocks or coral.

GLOSSARY

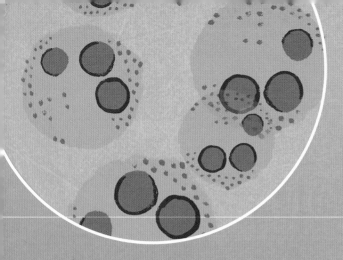

ALGAE Plural of alga, simple plants, such as seaweed, that have no real leaves, stems or roots. They grow in or near water.

BACTERIA Plural of bacterium, the simplest and smallest forms of life. Bacteria are found in air, water and soil, and also in living and dead animals and plants, and are often a cause of disease.

BIODEGRADE To be broken down by bacteria and other organisms.

BIODIVERSITY The variety of plant and animal life in a particular habitat.

BIOLUMINESCENCE The emission of light by animals such as deep-sea fish. The light is produced by chemical processes in the creature's body.

BUOYANT Able to keep afloat.

CARTILAGE Firm and flexible tissue, like soft bone, found in many animals.

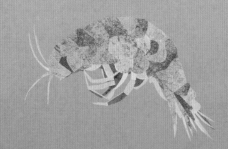

CRUSTACEAN A member of a large family of mainly aquatic animals that includes crabs, lobsters, shrimps and barnacles.

DETRITUS Waste.

ECHOLOCATION Finding objects using reflected sound; used by animals such as dolphins and whales.

ECOSYSTEM All the plants and living creatures in a particular area and their environment.

FOSSIL FUELS A fuel such as coal or oil formed millions of years ago from the remains of living creatures.

GELATINOUS Jelly-like.

GLOBAL WARMING A gradual increase in the overall temperature of the Earth, caused by increased levels of carbon dioxide, methane and other gases, which trap heat in the atmosphere.

GUYOT An undersea mountain with a flat top.

HABITAT The natural home or environment of an animal or plant.

INVERTEBRATE An animal that doesn't have a backbone, such as insects, squid and worms.

KEYSTONE SPECIES A species that has a bigger-than-average effect on its natural environment, helping maintain it and affecting many other species.

LARVA An insect at the stage when it has just come out of an egg.

MARINE SNOW The continuous shower of mostly organic matter that falls from the upper ocean to its deepest parts.

METABOLISM The chemical processes that happen inside an organism in order to maintain life.

MIGRATION A regular movement of animals from one region to another.

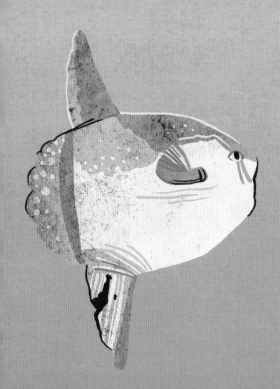

POLYP A phase in the life cycle of a jellyfish, or a small animal such as a sea anemone with a column-shaped body and a mouth at the top surrounded by a ring of tentacles.

SCAVENGER An animal that feeds on dead animals or plant matter.

SEAMOUNT An undersea mountain.

SERRATED Having a jagged edge.

SILHOUETTE The dark shape and outline of something that can be seen in low light.

STAGNANT Water with no current or flow, and no life.

SWIM BLADDER A gas-filled sac in the body of many bony fishes, used to control buoyancy.

MOLLUSC A member of a large family of soft-bodied animals that includes snails, slugs, mussels, squid and octopuses.

NUTRIENT A substance that keeps a living thing alive and helps it to grow.

ORGANIC MATTER Material composed of living or dead organisms.

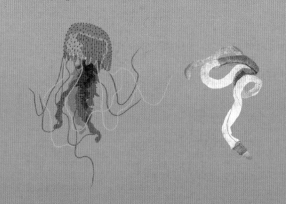

PHOTOSYNTHESIS The process by which plants use sunlight to obtain nutrients from carbon dioxide (CO_2) and water, and release oxygen.

PHYTOPLANKTON Plankton made up of plants or plant-like organisms.

SEDIMENT Matter that settles at the bottom of a body of water.

PLANKTON Small and microscopic organisms drifting in the sea, including algae, small crustaceans and the eggs and larvae of larger animals.

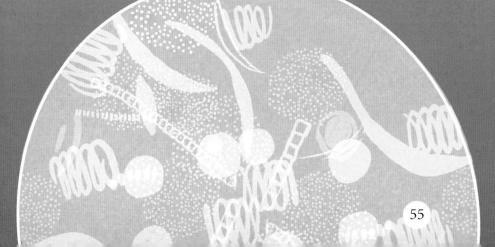

TRANSLUCENT Allowing light to pass through, but not completely clear.

ZOOPLANKTON Plankton consisting of small animals and the growing stages of larger animals.

INDEX